Also by Saskia Fraser

<u>Downloadable E-books</u>

Delicious Raw Food Desserts

5 Fun Steps to a High Raw

Christmas

Coming soon
In Print and all Ebook Formats

I'm Dreaming of Ice Cream The Raw
Revive 5-Day Detox
Raw Food for Winter

Saskia Fraser

Raw Freedom

Feel Great, Look Great

Quick and Delicious Raw Food Recipes for Everyday Energy

For Mark

With love and deep appreciation for all you do for us.

DISCLAIMER

The techniques and advice described in this book represent the opinions of the author, based on her experience. The author expressly disclaims any responsibility for any liability, loss or risk, personal or otherwise, which is incurred as a result of using any of the techniques, recipes or recommendations suggested herein. If in any doubt, or if requiring medical advice, please contact the appropriate health professional.

SIFIPUBLISHING
WWW.SIFIPUBLISHING.CO.UK

PV5 SP1

'Saskia has helped me understand the true source of vitality.' *Sarah Shaw*

'Her food will delight you, confound you, excite you.' *Catherine Stott*

'A really wonderful introduction into the possibilities of 'going raw'.' *Jeremy Coleman*

'Saskia is such a fantastic, living example of the diverse benefits of eating raw food. Her passion is contagious!' *Morag KcKillop*

'Saskia has made me think that the whole world should be zinging raw food into their cells.' *Debs Stanley*

CONTENTS

About Saskia

After a life changing accident in 2004, Saskia decided to leave behind the world of fashion to focus on healing her body, mind and spirit through raw foods. The powerful effects of her own healing journey ignited her passion for passing on this knowledge to those seeking deep physical wellbeing and a greater sense of purpose and connection in life. Through her work as a raw food mentor and life coach she has helped many hundreds of people to experience vibrant health, energy, calmness, intuitive focus and shining self-confidence.

In 2008, Saskia created Raw Freedom as a way to share her passion and knowledge about raw food. Through her coaching programmes, workshops, retreats and books she shows you how eating a high raw diet is not about denying your pleasures but about giving yourself the gift of good health, clear skin, shining eyes, a body to feel great about and loads more energy. Raw Food is an amazing catalyst for change on all levels, increasing self-knowledge whilst vastly improving your physical and emotional experience of life. Saskia is living proof of the power of raw food.

With love and thanks to Mark, Serena, Simon, Miranda, Nic, Lily, Barny, Lilah, Ben, Verity and Leo, for all your love, help and support. And to my clients, past, present and future, for being my inspiration.

Introduction

This recipe book has been a long time coming. Ever since I began teaching and coaching about raw food people have been asking me, 'Do you have a recipe book?' and finally I can answer, 'Yes, I do!'

This is a raw recipe book, but it's not about being 100% raw. It's about having access to a fabulously healthy way of eating that is practical and easy. I'm really excited to be sharing my quick and delicious raw food recipes with you in these pages. They hold the key to more energy, positivity and greater raw food confidence. Hurray for spreading the love of raw food!

Raw food for me is all about increasing vitality, clarity and emotional balance through a cleaner diet. Whether you are new to raw food or you are a full blown raw foodie, between these pages you will find dishes to delight your senses and expand the joy you experience in life. My motto is, 'Fall in love with life!' and these recipes will help you do just that.

I live in the UK. One of the most frustrating things about being into raw food in England is looking through amazing raw recipe books created in the United States. Unfortunately young coconut, jicama and other delicacies that are readily available in warmer climes aren't easily available here. So, the recipes you'll find in this book use ingredients found in cooler climes as well as hot ones.

When I create recipes my focus is always on making them:

1   Deliciously tasty

2   Quick to make

3   Using easy to find ingredients

4   And accessible to everyone (which means your granny, carnivorous husband and kids will love them too!)

I hope you will enjoy exploring this book, and I encourage you to set yourself the challenge of making 3 or more new recipes from it a week, for the next four weeks. Before you know it your raw food recipe repertoire will have expanded hugely and you'll be feeling amazing!

How to Use This Book

All the recipes in this book are easy. Some are really easy - chuck in the blender, press go, eat - others are easy but take a bit more time. Even the most involved recipes, like the cakes and tarts, shouldn't take more than 45 minutes from start to finish, plus maybe some setting time. Here are some simple things to know before you start:

1. Often with raw food recipes you will need to soak ingredients before using them, so make sure you read the recipe in advance.

2. I always recommend that the first time you make a recipe, you follow it carefully. It's a good idea to decide which recipes you want to make and shop for the right ingredients. There's also a whole chapter on what to do if you don't have the exact ingredients for a recipe.

3. Not all ingredients in this book are raw, but the vast majority are. If you regularly make recipes from these pages, you will reap the amazing rewards of eating a cleansing, rejuvenating and slimming raw food diet.

4 All the recipes are dairy-free, gluten-free, refined fat-free and refined sugar-free.

5 I am not vegan and so this is not a vegan recipe book, but most of the recipes are animal-product free. If you eat meat, fish, eggs and cheese and have no intention of giving them up, but would like to eat more healthily, I give suggestions of how to add them to the recipes, if it's relevant.

6 Buckwheat is not a type of wheat, but is actually a small, non-sweet fruit rather than a grain.

7 If you are not familiar with the measurements I use, refer to the Note on Terminology and Measures page.

A Note on Terminology and Measures

I am English, but I know that a lot of my readers will be from other countries. I've included a list of common words that are different in British English and American English, to help you understand what I'm talking about in the recipes if you're not familiar with British English.

ENGLISH	AMERICAN
Coriander	Cilantro
Aubergine	Eggplant
Pepper	Bell pepper
Beetroot	Beet
Courgette	Zucchini
Corn (on the cob)	Whole kernel-corn
Cling film	Saran wrap

I use all kinds of measurements in my recipes! Sometimes I find the British measurement system easiest, and other times the American system. Cup and spoon measures are easy to get hold of online and in kitchen shops everywhere these days. They are inexpensive and really quick to use as a measuring tool, so I think it's worth investing in a set.

Volume	Metric liquid / dry weight	Imperial
1 teaspoon	5ml	
1 tablespoon	15ml	
1/4 cup	60ml	
1/3 cup	85ml	
1/2 cup	125ml	
	140ml	1/4 pint
1 cup	250ml / 125g	4 1/2 oz
	285ml	1/2 pint
	550ml	1 pint
	0.5cm	1/4 inch
	1cm	1/2 inch
	2.5cm	1 inch

What's So Great About Raw Food?

People have experienced a multitude of health and life-enhancing effects from eating a high raw, nutrient rich diet. A 100% raw food diet isn't right for many people but, without being too extreme, eating an increased amount of cleansing and nutritious raw foods makes a world of difference to our energy levels, the strength of our immune system and the resilience and positivity of our emotional state.

Enzymes

According to research conducted by the renowned Doctor Edward Howell, enzymes play a large part in why raw food is so good for us. Food enzymes play an important role in the exchange between how much energy we get from the food we ingest, and how much energy it takes our bodies to digest and assimilate that food.

The theory according to Edward Howell goes like this:

There are 3 types of enzymes. Two of these

are essential to our metabolic function: metabolic enzymes and digestive enzymes. We have a finite store of these enzymes, which become depleted as we age. This depletion of metabolic and digestive enzymes is one of the causes of the aging process.

The third type of enzymes are food enzymes. Food enzymes are the live magic that make fruit and vegetables ripen. These enzymes are only found in raw foods that haven't been heated beyond 42 degrees centigrade or 107 degrees Fahrenheit. Cooking destroys 100% of food enzymes. As the name implies, these enzymes help our bodies to digest food. Digesting cooked food uses a lot of our body's vital energy. That's why, after a big Sunday roast, you'll feel sleepy. The body pulls energy away from your limbs and brain, channeling it to your digestive system to digest the heavy food that you've just eaten.

When you use raw ingredients that still contain their food enzymes, these food enzymes help your body to digest. Your body doesn't need to redirect energy from other areas to help with digestion, because there is already enough energy present. That's why, when you eat a raw meal or snack, your energy rises afterwards, rather than making you feel sluggish or sleepy.

Eating Clean Food

Over time we accumulate toxins in our bodies from the food and drink that we ingest, and from our environment. An excess of toxins in the body cause many symptoms, from lack of energy to severe illness. Toxins cause the blood to thicken. Through the metabolic process of diffusion, toxins are then moved into the intercellular fluid and then into our actual cells themselves. They cause our cell walls to thicken and become less supple, which in turn effects how efficiently our cells can do their work. Our cells become 'silted up'.

Our internal survival rests on our body's ability to maintain a narrow homeostasis (balance). A toxic system means it has to work much harder to maintain this balance, directing its precious energy into keeping toxic overload at bay rather than healing and regenerating our cells.

When you eat a clean diet you reverse this process. Your blood thins because it contains less toxins, allowing the toxins trapped in your body to move out of the intercellular fluid and cells, back into your blood. Once in the blood, they can be safely processed out of the body by the eliminatory organs, predominantly the liver and kidneys but also the skin, lungs and tongue.

Detox symptoms are caused by a backing up of toxins in the blood, i.e. when there are too many toxins in the blood for the eliminatory organs to handle. Detox symptoms can be relieved through re-thickening the blood with cooked foods, such as brown rice, or preferably through helping the body to release the toxins more quickly. Ways to help the body eliminate toxins more efficiently include:

- Drinking lots of water
- Exercising
- Sleeping
- Enemas and colonics
- Skin brushing

Strong detox symptoms usually pass within a day or two, with lesser detox symptoms continuing for longer.

Although detox symptoms can be a bit unsettling, it's important to remind yourself that they are happening because you are cleaning out your beautiful body. You are on the path to feeling fantastic!

Common detox symptoms include:

- Cold or hot flushes
- Cravings
- Bad breath
- Fevers
- Diarrhoea
- Wind
- Rashes
- Coughs
- Cold symptoms
- Drowsiness
- Headaches
- Aches & pains
- Nausea
- Unclear thinking
- Weight loss
- Light headedness
- Dark urine
- Spots and boils
- Dry skin
- Excess mucus
- Weakness
- Anxiety
- Depression
- Irritability
- Sadness
- Tearfulness

Where Does My
Protein Come From?

This is probably one of the most common questions I get asked. Raw food is in fact packed full of simple proteins (amino acids) and other nutrients which commonly are thought only to be found in animal products.

There are very few nutrients that can't be found on a raw vegan diet (namely Vitamins B12, K2 and D). If you are vegan, supplementing these vitamins is an important consideration for your long term health. If you are happy to eat a few eggs a week and a little unpasteurized cheese (or have no intention of giving up animal products) then this needn't concern you, unless you have a specific health issue that you are trying to heal.

If you 'go raw', the protein question is one that often gets asked by people who are sceptical of the health benefits of eating this way. It's good to be able to give them an answer! Whether you are vegan or not, it is interesting to know which raw foods are high in which nutrients.

Protein

- Sprouted pulses
- Dark green leafy veg
- Bee pollen
- Seaweed and algae
- Hemp seeds
- Maca
- Cacao
- Goji berries

Iron

- Spirulina
- Parsley
- Spinach
- Red fruit

- Dandelion leaves

Calcium

- Spirulina
- Green leafy veg
- Sesame seeds

Carbohydrates

- Fruit
- Sprouted pulses
- Sweet potatoes
- Squash
- Sweetcorn
- Raw buckwheat

- Sprouted quinoa

Omega Oils (EFAS/ Essential Fatty Acids)

- Hemp seeds
- Flax/Linseeds
- Pumpkin seeds
- Sunflower seeds
- Spirulina

What is a 'Raw Food Lifestyle'?

When it comes to answering this question, there are many differing schools of thought. Some people believe that the only way to truly experience all the fabulous rewards of raw food is to eat 100% raw, all of the time. Others believe that you can still reap the benefits by simply cleaning up your diet and replacing less healthy food choices with raw food alternatives. My philosophy lies somewhere in-between. I believe that everybody's raw food journey is different, and that what works for one person might not necessarily work for another. It's all about discovering what works best for you, your lifestyle and your body.

I admit that when I first discovered raw food, I'd frequently give myself a hard time if I fell off the raw food wagon and didn't stick to my goal of being 100% raw. I soon learnt that this approach just wasn't right for me. Once I gave myself permission to eat high raw, as opposed to 100% raw, it drastically improved both my life and my health. I realised that raw food doesn't have to be all or nothing. Eating a combination of raw and healthy cooked foods is much better than sliding down the slippery slope to eating mostly unhealthy cooked foods. With this approach, I have successfully given up my habitual unhealthy eating habits (and helped my coaching clients do the same), whilst still being able to enjoy the occasional coffee and cake, and having a few drinks at a party.

If you're wondering if the raw food lifestyle is right for you, ask yourself these three simple questions:

1 Do I want to feel full of vitality and positivity, and have a clear, focused mind?

2 Do I want to feel happy with how I look and feel great about my body?

3 Do I want to live in a way that is in harmony with our planet, and my body?

4 Do I want a sense of inner peace; mind, body and soul?

5 Do I want to look forward to the coming years with excitement and positivity?

If you answered 'Yes!' to any of these questions, then this highly energising and empowering way of nourishing yourself is right for you. One of the wonderful things about raw food is that it's so versatile. Literally anybody can incorporate it into their daily lives. If you're very busy and just want to include more raw food into your diet by using simple and easy recipes, you can. Equally, for people who are looking to get joyfully creative in the kitchen, there's a wealth of more involved recipes to try and lots of exotic and unusual ingredients to experiment with. The most important thing about the raw food lifestyle is that you live it in such a way that it makes you feel happier, healthier and more fulfilled in your daily life.

Can I Still Eat Cooked Food?

A lot of people think that in order to get the amazing benefits of eating raw food you can't eat cooked food. After 7 years of eating a high raw diet (this means I eat a lot of raw food, but not all raw food), I can tell you this is thankfully not true.

Discovering raw food radically changed how I view the idea of healthy eating. I used to think that I ate healthily because all my food was homemade (even if it was full of cream, sugar, meat etc.). After experiencing the amazing energy and mental positivity that comes with eating a high raw, low sugar, low dairy, low wheat, low meat (you get the idea!) diet, I now view 'healthy eating' as something quite different to 7 years ago.

Don't get me wrong, I enjoy the occasional pizza, coffee, cake and a hearty cooked meal from time to time, but cutting out the daily 'toxic' eating and drinking habits of my previous life has radically improved my health and wellbeing. I no longer drink tea or coffee everyday. Cheese is a rarity (when you taste the cashew 'cheese' in this book you'll see how you can cut down on the dairy kind), and fully cooked meals tend to happen when I go out for dinner or have the occasional vegetarian Sunday roast. The most important point to remember is to enjoy your food, whatever it is, and eat as much raw as possible. Being stressed whilst eating is not good for you. Love your food; love yourself!

So, the answer to 'Can I still eat cooked food?' is a resounding 'Yes'. My whole approach to raw food is about it being an accessible way to a longer, healthier and more joyful life. If that includes eating cooked food, great! I often have rice in the evenings, or toast (preferably wheat-free) with my raw soups. I've included what I call *crossover meal cooked additions*: cooked food suggestions to go with many of the raw recipes throughout this book. It makes it much easier to feed your friends and family raw food when you can add in some cooked food too. And sometimes you'll find you just don't want to eat raw. And that's okay! Just have a big green smoothie or juice the next morning, and get back on track.

I always recommend trying to use organic fruits and veggies whenever possible. If you are not vegan, one thing I will say, for the sake of your health and the health of our planet, is always try to get organic or wild meat and fish. You also want to make sure you buy organic cheeses that are made from goat or sheep's milk instead of cows' milk. Cows' milk is hard for humans to digest. Its molecular structure is 3 times the size of human milk, whilst both goat and sheep's milk are the same size as human milk, and therefore much easier for our bodies to process. Cow's milk has also been linked to asthma, eczema, arthritis, cancer and many more illnesses.

Raw food is not about denying yourself the pleasure of eating for the sake of good health (check out the desserts and treats in this book and you'll know what I mean!). It's about increasing your intake of highly nutritious foods and drinks so that you can be your best self, physically, mentally and emotionally. The most important lesson that I've learnt during my raw food journey is to love myself, whatever I eat. Give up punishing yourself mentally for eating chocolate and cake. Learn how to make chocolate and cake that's actually good for you instead!

Making Food for Family and Friends

Once you start to experience all the fabulous rewards of eating raw food, it's usual to want to share your new found health and happiness with family and friends. This isn't always easy. If your loved ones are used to more traditional food choices, it's common to be faced with scepticism or concerns about your health and wellbeing. If you have kids, they may well refuse to eat raw at first. Don't worry! There are simple tips and tricks for making it easier, and ways of normalising the idea of raw food for everyone.

It's important to understand that, for those who are unfamiliar with raw food, it can at first seem faddy, extreme or just plain impractical. In my experience, one of the best ways to reassure people is by getting them to taste how delicious raw food is. There is often no need to mention it's raw at all!

There are two ways that I've found particularly successful when it comes to sharing raw food. The first, for adults, is to put on a raw food dinner party. I personally like to make a variety of smaller dishes to create a raw food mezze-style meal. This gives people the opportunity to try an array of new tastes and flavours and also gives you a chance to have fun in the kitchen. By preparing lots of smaller dishes, you can also ensure you make something that'll suit everybody's tastes.

The second way, for kids as well as adults, is to, a) introduce them to raw food a little at a time (start with easy, fruit based smoothies and salads using their favourite vegetables and fruit), b) put a combination of raw and cooked dishes on the table and let everyone help themselves, c) be patient! It can often take kids and some adults (like meat-and-2-veg husbands) up to a year to become accustomed to raw food and to see it as a normal food choice.   Children are especially responsive to trying new things. Raw food treats, chocolates and desserts are guaranteed to be a sure-fire hit with every age group!

It's so easy to make raw food look mouth-wateringly gorgeous, with all of its vibrant colours and diverse textures. The recipes in this book are here to show you how to do exactly that. It's packed full of delicious and super quick raw food recipes that you'll want to make again and again, for yourself, your family and your friends.

So, whether you choose to make my scrummy pea and mint soup, legendary lime and kiwi cheesecake or deliciously decadent raw chocolate spread, you'll find that once your loved ones have experienced some of the tantalising tastes and exotic flavours for themselves, they'll be far more understanding and supportive as you continue your discovery of raw food. And who knows, you might even convert one or two of them along the way!

Raw Food Kitchen Equipment

One of the reservations that many people have when it comes to raw food is the belief that you need lots of expensive and fancy kitchen equipment in order to prepare recipes. The reality is that it's nowhere near as complicated as people tend to think. In fact, the likelihood is that you already have most of what you need in your kitchen. When I first started on my raw food journey, I made all my raw food using a knife, a chopping board and a blender. I had no problem in finding delicious raw food recipes that I could prepare.

To begin with, it's not necessary to spend a lot of money on a good quality blender; a hand blender is more than enough to get you started. As a beginner, the following equipment is all you'll really need:

- Sharp knives - If you're looking to eat more healthily you can guarantee that you'll be chopping, so a sharp knife is going to save you a lot of time and effort. You can get really easy-to-use knife sharpeners these days, so do yourself a favour and get one.
- Hand-held or wand blender

- Sprouting jars - for growing your own nutrition-packed raw sprouts.
- Measuring cups and spoons - most raw food recipes use these as a standard way of measuring ingredients.
- Measuring jug
- Mixing bowls
- Peeler, crusher, grater etc. - your standard kitchen gadgets.
- Weighing machine

With this equipment, you can make everything from high energy raw salads, right through to fruit crumbles, chocolate and raw food cheesecake.

When you know that raw food is something that you want to embrace long-term as part of your everyday diet, it's well worth thinking about investing in a high speed blender and other good-quality kitchen equipment. A really good blender speeds up your food preparation quite considerably. It allows you to make some of my raw food favourites, such as smoothies, pâtés, soups and desserts, in a matter of minutes. It's much easier to stay on the raw food path when you can make your recipes quickly, and it's most fun when you have equipment that allows you to get really creative.

A fully equipped raw food kitchen like mine will also include:

- Juicer - with this you can make incredibly nutritious and energising drinks that are easier and quicker to digest than smoothies. With high bio-availability, juices are a great source of nutrients for everybody, but particularly good for those suffering with skin ailments or digestive problems.
- High speed blender - brilliant for making smoothies on the go. You can easily whip up a silky smoothie in no time at all, as well as pâtés, sauces, soups, desserts, savoury fillings and dehydrator mixes.
- Food processor - takes the hassle out of chopping, slicing and grating. Perfect for energy balls, sweet and savoury tart crusts, as well as chunkier dehydrator mixes.
- Dehydrator - makes crackers, biscuits, dried fruit, raw bread, pizza bases, breakfast cereals and vegetable crisps. It can also warm raw recipes for you when you're in the mood for some hot-food comfort.
- Vegetable spiralizer - makes raw pasta and spaghetti; perfect for lovers of healthy Italian food!
- Mandolin - for finely slicing and chopping fresh fruit and vegetables.
- Chefs rings, cake and tart tins - for making desserts, cakes and savoury tarts.
- Pastry cutter - for making biscuits and crackers.

- Citrus zester - for quickly zesting lime, orange, lemon and grapefruit for garnishes and recipes.
- Nut milk bag - for straining nut and seed milks. Jelly bags, usually used for preserving, make really good nut milk bags. If you don't have one of these, you can use a muslin cloth or clean tea towel instead.
- Piping bag - for icings and decorations.

Having a kitchen stocked with this list of equipment makes a greater choice of recipes easy, beautiful and fun to make. You'll literally have a whole world of raw food recipes at your fingertips!

A Note on Ingredients

I know people often get frustrated with the fact that a lot of raw recipes use hard to find ingredients. I come from the UK and many raw recipes are written for an American audience. It's hard to find green coconuts, jicama and other such specialist foods in the UK, but it doesn't mean you have to be restricted with what you can make if you live in colder climes. You'll find that the recipes in this book all use easy to find ingredients, wherever you are in the world. However, if you can't find an ingredient at your local health food shop or supermarket, you will be able to buy it online.

I recommend that you follow a recipe closely the first time you make it. This is a good way to familiarise yourself with the taste and flavour of different raw ingredients. The magic flavours of raw food are often in the alchemy and specific ratios of a recipe. After you've made it once with the ingredients I give you, if you want to make it again but don't have everything you need, don't let that stop you. If you can think of something that has a similar flavour or texture, you can replace it! However, if ever you're in doubt, just follow the simple guidelines on the following pages.

Nuts and Seeds

You'll notice that in a lot of my recipes it says to soak the nuts and seeds. The reason for doing this is to remove the less digestible enzyme inhibitors, which hold them dormant and stop them growing into plants. Soaking, therefore, begins the nut and seed's journey to becoming a plant, and it becomes more nutritious simply from a night of soaking. Once soaked, they have a much shorter shelf life and don't work in recipes that you want to last more than a day or two.

When it comes to recipes, nuts and seeds are all interchangeable, e.g. if you don't have almonds, use Brazil nuts or sunflower seeds. The harder the nut, the grainier the texture, if you're blending. If you want a smooth texture use cashews, hulled hemp seeds or other seeds. The rule here is that anything goes, so have fun mixing it up!

Remember, if you're using them in a blended recipe, just be aware that it will change the colour and the flavour of the food.

Fruits

If your fruit bowl doesn't happen to have the fruit mentioned in a recipe, just use a different but similar fruit instead. You can use limes instead of lemons; grapefruits instead of oranges; blueberries instead of strawberries; or apples instead of pears, etc.

Vegetables

Vegetables that are easily interchangeable in a recipe are root veg (you can substitute carrots for sweet potato, butternut squash for celeriac, etc), and dark green leafy veg (you can replace spinach with Swiss chard, or use kale instead of broccoli, etc.)

Herbs and Spices

Herbs and spices are often what make the difference between a recipe tasting 'okay' and downright delicious. I generally don't mess around with the herbs and spices in a recipe but here's a few exceptions:

- Fresh oregano and thyme are good substitutes for each other.
- Fresh basil and parsley can be used in place of each other.
- Ground coriander can be switched for ground cumin or ground ginger, and paprika can be used as a mild replacement for chilli.
- Garlic can be used instead of spring onion, or vice versa.
- Lime zest is a good substitute for kaffir lime leaves.
- Lemon zest can be used if you can't get hold of lemon grass.

Sweeteners

Most people find they have a preferred sweetener, largely depending on individual dietary requirements and personal taste. Unless your sweetener is still in its natural state, it's relevant to remember that it has been processed, either using heat or techniques that expose them to oxidisation. I think of all sweeteners as luxury foods rather than foods I want to use everyday.

You might choose to opt for a vegan-friendly sweetener, or need one with a low GI (glycemic index), or you might simply discover a sweetener that you prefer the taste of. My sweeteners of choice are honey and raw agave syrup, but you can replace the sweeteners in my recipes with:

- Date paste (made from fresh dates and water)
- Maple syrup (not raw, but packed full of minerals so go for the high grade variety)
- Xylitol (not raw and quite processed, but low G.I.)
- Raw palm sugar
- Raw agave syrup
- Honey
- Raw coconut sugar

Healthy Fats

There are 3 different categories of healthy raw food fats:

- Liquid fats, which are your oils - 'extra virgin' means it hasn't been heat treated during extraction, so buy your oils extra virgin whenever possible.
- Solid fats, such as raw cacao butter, and coconut oil if you live in a colder country.
- Whole foods containing healthy fats, such as avocados, nuts and seeds.

Within each of these categories, you can swap ingredients around. If you don't have olive oil, use hemp oil or sunflower oil.

If you don't have raw cacao butter, use coconut oil. Be mindful that coconut oil will soften more quickly than raw cacao butter at room temperature, so if you're eating raw chocolate made with coconut oil you'll have to lick your fingers afterwards!

In blended recipes, such as soups and smoothies, you can substitute cashews with avocado, or vice versa. Cashews are richer and heavier than avocado and both are deliciously creamy.

Most importantly, learn to trust your own instincts about what will taste good and have fun getting creative in the kitchen!

Salt

You'll notice that the salt in my recipes is 'mineral salt'. What I mean by mineral salt is either Himalayan pink salt or an unrefined sea salt. A lot of the sea salts you'll find on the supermarket shelves have had the minerals (i.e. their goodness) washed out of them, in order to make them white. Check sea salt before buying it, to make sure it still contains its full range of minerals.

Superfoods

Superfoods are not necessary but I enjoy them as an extra health-boost. Maca is an Andean root related to radish, and has been used for hundreds of years as an adaptogen, helping to balance hormones. Spirulina and chlorella are high in essential fatty acids and protein, helping to keep your brain functioning well. Bee pollen is high in B vitamins, protein, and if you can get hold of the fresh-frozen variety, is anti-fungal, and antibacterial to boot.

Raw raw cacao is also considered a superfood because it is incredibly high in minerals. However, a word of caution: it is also a powerful stimulant - great if you need to stay up late working, not so great if you want to get to sleep early! Don't let this put you off, just remember that raw cacao should be a treat, not a daily staple.

The Recipes

Green Smoothies & Juices

'Green smoothies and juices are the elixir of life.'

The great thing about green smoothies is that they're so simple to make - it's literally just a case of blend and go! So, if like me, you lead a super busy life, they're a great way of getting the nourishment your body needs without sacrificing time you don't have to spare. They're high in chlorophyll, which converts sunlight into usable energy, and packed full of live enzymes that help the body's digestive processes.

Green leafy vegetables should be a fundamental part of your diet. They contain high amounts of essential minerals including iron, calcium, potassium and magnesium. Dark green leafy veg such as kale and spinach are also high in protein, and a great source of dietary fibre. Most people don't eat enough greens, so green smoothies and juices are a brilliant way of easily incorporating these amazing veggies into your diet. Both refreshing and revitalising, they're a delicious and satisfying way to better health and more energy.

My Top 15 Greens

- Kale
- Spinach
- Lettuce
- Rocket
- Watercress
- Celery
- Fennel
- Broccoli
- Chard
- Cabbage
- Parsley
- Coriander
- Basil
- Dandelion
- Chickweed

To Juice or To Smoothie?

Smoothies are super quick to make and will fill you up for longer because they contain lots of fibre. The fibre in smoothies slows down oxidation, which means that you can put your smoothie in an airtight flask with a few cubes of ice and it will retain much of its goodness for a good few hours.

Juices take more preparation time, but pack a bigger nutritional punch than smoothies, so it's well worth the extra effort. Because they contain very little fibre they're easier for the body to absorb, allowing you to benefit from the maximum amount of nourishing goodness. Juices are at their most nutritionally powerful when they are fresh, before oxidation starts to degrade the nutrients. To get the most from your juice, drink it right after you make it.

There are endless combinations of ingredients and flavours to try. This chapter contains some of my favourite tried and tested recipes. Remember to mix it up and try different ones frequently, rather than just sticking to the same one or two. This will ensure that you benefit from a broad spectrum of vitamins and minerals.

Even if you introduce just one or two of these delicious recipes a day, and change nothing else in your diet, you will notice an improvement in your overall health and energy levels. They're Mother Nature's very own multivitamin!

Blue Green Super Smoothie

When avocados are in season this is one of my daily staples. It's great for taking to work in a flask with a few cubes of ice. It makes the perfect mid-morning snack too.

Equipment: knife, chopping board, blender
Makes 1 large glass

300ml of water
1 ripe banana, peeled
½ a ripe avocado, peel and stone removed
½ teaspoon of spirulina
½ teaspoon of maca
½ teaspoon of bee pollen
1 pinch of mineral salt
raw agave syrup or honey to taste (optional)

Blend all the ingredients together until smooth, adding more water to achieve a consistency that pleases you. Keep this smoothie cold and drink it within 6 hours.

Pear, Lettuce & Mint Smoothie

A refreshing start to your day, or a lovely pick-me-up mid-afternoon, this smoothie is particularly good in the summer because of its light freshness, and in autumn when pears are at their best.

Equipment: knife, chopping board, blender
Makes 1 large glass

300ml water
5 big leaves of green lettuce
3 ripe pears
mint to taste (I like a good handful)

Core the pears and blend all the ingredients together until smooth. Add more water to achieve your desired consistency and drink within half an hour to get the most goodness from it.

Immunity Smoothie

When you're in need of some immune system support, this yummy and unusual smoothie can help you avoid or overcome pesky colds, sore throats and coughs.

Equipment: knife, chopping board, blender
Makes 1 large glass

2 handfuls of spinach or other dark green leafy veg
2 oranges, peeled
1 pear
1cm of fresh ginger
1 teaspoon of ground cinnamon
1 teaspoon of ground coriander
½ teaspoon of turmeric
300ml of water

Core your pears and remove any pips from the oranges. Blend all the ingredients together until smooth and creamy. Add more water for your desired consistency and drink within half an hour to reap the most nutritional benefit from it.

Almond Superfood Smoothie

This is a delicious smoothie that I often have pre or post exercising. It's packed full of protein and superfoods to help replenish energy and heal tired muscles. It's another great one for putting in a flask with a few cubes of ice to take to work or to travel with.

Equipment: blender
Makes 1 large glass

500ml of almond milk (see p.78)
1 teaspoon of maca
1 teaspoon of bee pollen
1 teaspoon of raw cacao powder
¼ teaspoon of spirulina or green superfood powder
1-2 teaspoons of raw agave syrup or honey (optional)

Blend all the ingredients together. Keep cold and drink within 6 hours.

Orange, Mango & Spinach Smoothie

I was inspired to make this smoothie on a cold autumn day when I felt the need for some sunshine in my mouth and a boost against the colds that often come with the change of seasons. I love its tropical flavour.

Equipment: knife, chopping board, blender
Makes 1 large glass

1 mango
1 banana, peeled
3 oranges, peeled and pips removed
1cm of fresh ginger
2 handfuls of spinach

Remove the skin and stone from the mango and blend all the ingredients together until smooth. For the best health benefits drink your smoothie soon after making it.

Pear & Chocolate Smoothie

This is an unusual combination that really works for those of us that like fruit and chocolate together. The cardamom gives a deliciously sophisticated and aromatic warmth to this smoothie.

Equipment: knife, chopping board, blender, pestle and mortar (optional)
Makes 1 large glass

2 ripe pears, cored
1 teaspoon of raw cacao powder
2 handfuls of baby leaf spinach
2 cardamoms
150ml of water

Remove the cardamoms from their husks and grind with a pestle and mortar or the back of a wooden spoon on a chopping board. Blend together with the rest of the ingredients, until smooth. For the best flavour and to get the most from this smoothie drink it within half an hour of making it.

Mango & Spinach Smoothie

This raw food classic is a super quick and delicious way of getting your greens in without tasting them. It's brilliant for adults and kids alike.

Equipment: knife, chopping board, blender
Makes 1 large glass

300ml of water
3 handfuls of spinach
1 ripe mango

Remove the skin and stone from the mango and blend all the ingredients together until smooth. Add more water to achieve your desired consistency. Pour into a large glass and drink within half an hour of making to get the most goodness out of it.

Pineapple Coriander Smoothie

One of my all-time favourite smoothies! People tend to think of coriander as a savoury flavour, but it works brilliantly with tropical fruits too.

Equipment: knife, chopping board, blender
Makes 1 large glass

½ a pineapple, peeled and cored
1 handful of coriander leaves
1cm of fresh ginger
½ lime, juice of
300ml of water

Blend all your ingredients together until you've got a lovely smooth drink. Add more water if it's too thick for you, and drink soon after making.

Classic Green Juice

This is the juice I have most days. You can literally feel the goodness zinging into your cells as you're drinking. If you're not used to green juices, start off with one handful of dark green leafy veg and graduate to two handfuls once you are used to the taste.

Equipment: knife, chopping board, juicer
Makes 1 large glass

2 handfuls of kale, or other dark green leafy veg such as spinach or chard
3 sticks of celery
3 apples
¼ lime, with peel on

Remove the stalks from the apples and juice all your ingredients together. Enjoy drinking it straight away for the best taste and to get the most goodness from it.

Pink Grapefruit & Mint Juice

The colour alone has me falling in love with this juice every time I make it. If you've got a juicer that can handle citrus fruits (usually the centrifugal type), remove the skin and then juice the whole grapefruit, pith, pips an' all. Otherwise, juice the grapefruits by hand first.

Equipment: knife, chopping board, juicer (and a citrus squeezer if you're juicer isn't very good with soft fruits)
Makes 1 large glass

2 pink grapefruits
1 handful of fresh mint

Remove the peel from the grapefruits and juice all your ingredients together. Enjoy drinking it straight away for the best taste and most goodness.

Summer Sunshine Juice

Oh, wow! I can't wait for you to taste this beauty of a juice. I created it for our regular Ready, Steady, Juice day and make it whenever strawberries are in season (and sometimes even when they are not because it's so good!).

Equipment: knife, chopping board, juicer
Makes 1 large glass

4 apples
10 strawberries
2 sticks of celery
2 handfuls of lettuce
¼ lime, with peel on

Remove any stalks from the apples and leave the green leaves on the strawberries. Juice all your ingredients together and enjoy drinking it straight away for the best taste and to get the most goodness from it.

Green Soother Juice

This is a lovely light, refreshing green juice that's easy on the taste buds. If you're a beginner with green juices or don't feel like a full-power green juice, this one hits the spot.

Equipment: knife, chopping board, juicer
Makes 1 large glass

3 hard pears
½ cucumber
1 courgette
½ lettuce
¼ lemon, with peel on

Cut the stalks off the pears. Top and tail the cucumber and courgette. Juice all your ingredients together and enjoy drinking it straight away for the best taste and to get the most goodness from it.

Full of Light Vegetable Juice

I think everyone should learn to love vegetable juice. It's very easy to end up having a lot of sweet fruit, especially in juices. Unless you're doing lots of physical exercise and can burn the fruit sugar off, I tend to recommend that you keep to a maximum of 3 pieces of fruit a day, except for special occasions.

Equipment: knife, chopping board, juicer
Makes 1 large glass

2 handfuls of sugar snap peas
4 celery sticks
1 fennel bulb
½ cucumber
1 handful of fresh mint
½ lime, with peel on

Juice all your ingredients together and enjoy drinking it straight away for the best taste and to get the most goodness from it.

Heavenly Vegetable Juice

This lush vegetable juice is deeply satisfying. If you've never tried spring onion or garlic in a juice before, this is a gentle juicy introduction to a very healing plant family.

Equipment: knife, chopping board, juicer
Makes 1 large glass

4 tomatoes
6 carrots
½ cucumber
2 handfuls of fresh parsley
1 handful of fresh basil
1 spring onion
½ lime, with peel on

Juice all your ingredients together and enjoy drinking it straight away for the best taste and to get the most goodness from it.

Breakfast

'Raw food breakfasts rock! They are satisfying, quick and super tasty. Eat a raw breakfast and you'll be starting your day with the most healthy and energising food possible.'

It's often said that breakfast is the most important meal of the day. This is certainly true when it comes to raw food. Your body starts its cleansing phase whilst you sleep, and continues until you literally 'break the fast' with your first meal of the day. This is why, to have your body working as efficiently as possible, it's important to eat a breakfast that's easy to digest and as alkaline as possible. Starting with a healthy breakfast will kick-start your day, providing you with plenty of energy and helping to alkalise your system. Alkalising your system is important because over-acidity has been linked to pretty much all major illnesses and health complaints.

Some people find that a green smoothie or juice is the best way to start their morning. Others wake feeling ravenous and find they need a more filling breakfast to get them through the day. There's no right or wrong way - it's all about finding what works best for you. The most important thing is to eat a healthy breakfast that helps you to wake naturally each morning, and jump out of bed feeling full of vitality and energy.

All the breakfast recipes in this chapter are easy to make the night before, so you can cut down your preparation time in the morning and take them to work. Store them in the fridge at work and they'll be ready and waiting for whenever you get hungry. As with standard breakfasts, raw breakfasts can be sweet or savoury. I often have a raw 'breakfast' as a mid-afternoon snack, a light supper, or even as a tasty dessert, so don't be afraid to mix it up.

Some Good Things to Know

If you're not taking regular exercise, try to limit your fruit intake to 1-3 pieces a day (a handful of dried fruit counts as two pieces). Sugar, including too much fruit sugar, is acidic for the body and can drain your energy and hinder good health. If you're trying to lose weight or are insulin resistant, it's better to limit your intake of fruit sugars until you've reached your ideal weight or your health improves.

If you are exercising regularly, you can afford to increase your fruit intake because your body burns up the sugars. For pre and post-workout, the breakfast recipes containing raw buckwheat are particularly good. They contain an alkaline form of protein as well as carbohydrate, which helps with muscle building and speeding up recovery.

Almond Milk

With this recipe you can substitute the almonds for other nuts or seeds, or a combination of both. Some of my favourite combinations are hazelnut and hemp milk, or almond and pumpkin seed milk. If you're new to nut milks, plain almond is a great one to start with because it has a subtle flavour. If you are used to full fat milk, then use 2 parts water for a rich and creamy milk. If you are used to dairy-free alternatives, like soya milk or rice milk, it's likely you'll find using 3-5 parts water rich enough for you.

Equipment: blender, muslin cloth/jelly bag/clean tea towel
Makes 500ml (2 cups) – 1250ml (5 cups)

1 cup of almonds, soaked for at least 8 hours or overnight
2 - 5 parts water (i.e. 3-5 cups)

Rinse the almonds thoroughly. Blend the almonds with the water until the almonds are finely ground. Strain the mixture through a muslin, jelly bag or clean tea towel, squeezing all the milk through into a bowl or jug.

Your almond milk is now ready to use in a smoothie, on your muesli, and in raw soups. Or just drink its deliciously healthy creaminess as it is!

Nut and seed milks keep in the fridge for 24 hours.

Alfalfa Muesli

This is a favourite at my workshops. Most people start off sceptical at the thought of alfalfa sprouts for breakfast, but once they've tasted this recipe it becomes a breakfast staple because it's so delicious and good for you.

Equipment: knife, chopping board, blender for the almond milk
Makes one bowl

1 handful of alfalfa sprouts
fruits of your choice (e.g. mango, fresh fig and strawberry), cut into bite size pieces
1 handful of seeds of your choice (e.g. sunflower and pumpkin seeds)
fresh almond milk (see p.78)
raw agave syrup or honey (optional)

Thoroughly mix the alfalfa sprouts with your fruit in a breakfast bowl. Scatter your seeds over the top and pour over the almond milk. If you want, you can add raw agave syrup or honey to taste.

Best eaten on the day of making but it will keep in the fridge for 24 hours.

Buckwheat Muesli

Buckwheat is fabulous! It's alkalising and contains carbohydrate and protein, making it brilliant for a filling breakfast. The ginger and mint adds a hint of sophistication.

Equipment: knife, chopping board
Makes one bowl

1 cup of raw buckwheat
1 handful of raisins
1 pinch of mineral salt
500ml of water

Mix together the buckwheat, raisins, salt and water and leave to soak overnight.

½ cm of fresh ginger, grated
1 teaspoon of finely chopped mint leaves
1 banana, peeled and sliced
berries (optional)
nut/seed milk (see p.78) or juice (both optional)

Rinse your soaked buckwheat and raisin mix until the water runs clear. Put it in your breakfast bowl.

Stir the ginger and mint through your muesli and top with chopped fruit. If you like more liquid in your muesli add nut/seed milk or juice.

Best eaten on the day of making but it will keep in the fridge for 24 hours.

Fruit Salad & Cream

Simple but oh-so-gorgeous! Unless you absolutely love apples, leave them out. Treat yourself to your favourite fruit, all in one bowl.

Equipment: knife, chopping board, blender
Makes one bowl

Make a delicious fruit salad from a selection of the following fruit:

banana, papaya, strawberries, blueberries, raspberries, mango, grapes, pear, nectarine, dates, pineapple, orange, plums, figs

Cream
1 handful of cashew nuts
1 orange, juice of
2 medjool dates, pitted

Blend the nuts with the orange juice and dates, adding water if necessary to get a creamy consistency.

Pour over your fruit salad and indulge!

Best eaten on the day of making but it will keep in the fridge for 24 hours.

Ginger and Mint Fruit Salad

This sophisticated take on a classic fruit salad is great for breakfast or as a light and easy pudding. The ginger adds warmth when the weather is not so summery but you still feel like fruit.

Equipment: knife, chopping board
Makes one bowl

Make a delicious fruit salad for one from a selection of the following fruit:

banana, papaya, strawberries, blueberries, raspberries, mango, grapes, pear, nectarine, dates, pineapple, orange, plums, figs

Add

4 mint leaves, finely chopped
½ cm of fresh ginger, finely chopped or grated

Mix all your ingredients together well. When you sit down to eat this delicious breakfast, close your eyes and really savor the flavours.

Best eaten on the day of making but it will keep in the fridge for 24 hours.

Omega Sweet Sprinkle

This health-packed sprinkle is a tasty way of getting more essential fatty acids into your diet. Lubricate your joints and feed your brain with a couple of tablespoons of this every day. It needs to be eaten fresh, before the delicate oils have a chance to oxidise and lose their nutrients. Sprinkle 2-6 tablespoons over breakfasts, salads, puddings, smoothies and raw ice cream.

Equipment: spice grinder, coffee mill or small food processor
Makes 2 days' worth

2 tablespoons of golden flaxseeds
1 tablespoon of poppy seeds
1 tablespoon of sesame seeds
2 tablespoons of goji berries

Grind all the ingredients together. Store in an airtight container in the fridge and use within 2-3 days.

Superfood Porridge

When you feel like comfort food in the morning, this porridge hits the spot. It's full of nutritious, tasty seeds and fruit to kick start your day.

Equipment: knife, chopping board, knife, blender
Makes one bowl

½ cup of raw buckwheat, soaked overnight
1 handful of pumpkin seeds, soaked overnight
1 handful of sunflower seeds, soaked overnight
1 handful of goji berries, soaked in 60ml of water, overnight
2 tablespoons of hulled (white) hemp seeds (optional)
1 teaspoon of bee pollen (optional)
1 handful of fresh fruit (e.g. peach and strawberry)

The night before, put the buckwheat, pumpkin and sunflower seeds in plenty of water to soak overnight. In a separate container, soak the goji berries in a quarter cup of water.

In the morning, rinse the buckwheat and seeds. Blend them with the goji berries and the goji berry soak water.

Put the porridge in your breakfast bowl and top with fresh fruit, adding bee pollen and hulled hemp seeds if you have them.

Keeps for 24 hours in the fridge.

Apple Cinnamon Porridge

Apple and cinnamon is a classic combination that I love. Cinnamon balances blood sugar so it's a great start to the day, particularly if you experience blood sugar highs and lows.

Equipment: knife, chopping board, blender, grater
Makes one bowl

1 handful of almonds, soaked overnight and then rinsed
½ cup of raw buckwheat, soaked overnight and then rinsed
1 small handful of raisins, soaked separately overnight in 120ml of water
1 teaspoon of ground cinnamon
1 small pinch of mineral salt
1 apple, grated
honey or raw agave syrup to taste (optional)

Blend the soaked and rinsed almonds and buckwheat with 3 tablespoons of the raisin soak water, cinnamon, honey/raw agave and salt until smooth and creamy.

Put the mixture into a bowl, stir through the raisins and top with grated apple.

This porridge is great with some fresh ginger too!

Keeps for 24 hours in the fridge.

Mango Cardamom Porridge

For those of us who are mango lovers, what a treat! I'm all for breakfast being a taste sensation, and starting the day with something as satisfying and yummy as this porridge always makes me happy.

Equipment: knife, chopping board, blender
Makes one bowl

1 cup of raw buckwheat, soaked overnight & then rinsed
3 cardamom pods, soaked overnight
1 teaspoon of raw agave syrup or honey
1 small pinch of mineral salt
½ cm of fresh ginger (optional)
1 mango, skin and stone removed
A sprinkling of chia seeds (optional)

Remove the cardamom seeds from their pods. Blend the soaked and rinsed buckwheat with three quarters of the mango, the cardamom seeds, ginger, raw agave and salt until smooth and creamy.

Put your creamy porridge into a bowl and top with the remaining chopped mango and chia seeds.

Keeps for 24 hours in the fridge.

Banana Coconut Porridge

I am a great fan of coconut and in this recipe it gives the porridge its 'sweetness'. If you are on a low fruit-sugar diet, you can have this without the banana.

Equipment: knife, chopping board, blender
Makes one bowl

1 handful of almonds, soaked overnight & then rinsed
½ cup of raw buckwheat, soaked overnight & then rinsed
3 tablespoons of desiccated coconut, soaked in ½ cup of water for at least 1 hour or overnight
1 small pinch of mineral salt
1 teaspoon of raw agave syrup or honey (optional)
½ cm of fresh ginger (optional)
1 banana, peeled and sliced

Blend the soaked and rinsed almonds and buckwheat with the coconut, coconut soak water, ginger, raw agave and salt until smooth and creamy. Put the mixture into a bowl and top with sliced banana.

Note: Great with some raw cacao powder blended in too.

Keeps for 24 hours in the fridge.

Avocado Tomato Basil Breakfast

I love this as a weekend breakfast or if I'm feeling like something savoury in the morning. My sister loves this breakfast with a poached egg on top.

Equipment: knife, chopping board
Serves 1

1 avocado
2 tomatoes
5-8 basil leaves
extra virgin olive oil
1 pinch of mineral salt
¼ lime
ground black pepper (optional)

Cut the avocado in half length ways and remove the stone. While it's still in its skin, cut the avocado flesh into slices, without cutting through the skin. Scoop your avocado slices out in one go with a spoon.

Slice the tomatoes thinly.

Arrange the avocado in a fan shape, layer the tomatoes over the top and then sprinkle with the basil leaves.

Drizzle olive oil over the whole lot, and sprinkle with salt and pepper. Squeeze the lime over the top to finish.

Keep in the fridge and eat on the day of making.

Mushrooms on Toast

This is such a versatile recipe I often find myself having it lots of times in one week. I love marinated mushrooms for breakfast, as I've suggested here, or on top of a big salad for lunch. They are also delicious with raw pasta dishes.

Equipment: knife, chopping board
Serves 1

4 brown mushrooms or 1 portobello mushroom
4 tablespoons of extra virgin olive oil
1 tablespoon of tamari or nama shoyu
black pepper to taste (optional)
1 or 2 raw crackers or a slice of wheat-free toast

Whisk the olive oil and nama shoyu or tamari in a bowl until they are thoroughly combined. Slice the mushrooms and toss them in the oil and tamari, making sure each slice is completely covered in the sauce. Leave to marinade for at least 30 minutes, in an airing cupboard or dehydrator if you have one.

Drain the marinade and serve your mushrooms on top of raw crackers or wheat-free toast.

Any leftover marinade is delicious used in salad dressings.

Herb Courgette on Toast

I love the look of peeled courgette, with its delicate colours and ribbon texture. This is a great breakfast when you're feeling like something a bit more substantial.

Equipment: knife, chopping board, peeler
Serves 1

1 small courgette, topped and tailed
2 tablespoons of extra virgin olive oil
1 large pinch of mineral salt
¼ lemon, juice and zest
1 teaspoon of dried oregano or 2 teaspoons of fresh oregano
black pepper to taste (optional)
10 pitted green olives, halved
1 slice of wheat-free toast or 1 raw cracker (optional)

Peel the courgette into ribbons and place in a bowl with the olives, oregano, olive oil, salt, pepper and lemon juice and zest.

Mix thoroughly and leave to marinade for at least 30 minutes.

Drain the marinade and serve on a raw cracker or wheat-free toast.

You can use any left-over marinade in salad dressings.

Keeps in the fridge for 24 hours, without the crackers or toast.

Wilted Greens with Sweet Chilli Sauce

This is my raw equivalent of a fry up. You can have it simply with raw sweet chilli sauce, or you can add marinated mushrooms and poached eggs for a heartier breakfast.

Equipment: knife, chopping board, blender
Serves 1

For the Wilted Greens

3 generous handfuls of rainbow chard, chard or spinach
½ clove of garlic, crushed or finely chopped
3 tablespoons of extra virgin olive oil
1 large pinch of mineral salt

Chop your greens into 1cm strips (you can bunch them all together to make this quicker). Put your chopped greens in a large bowl with the olive oil, salt and garlic. Massage the mixture firmly between your fingers until the greens soften and wilt (approximately 5 minutes). Set them to one side while you make the chilli sauce.

Sweet Chilli Sauce

2 large, medium spicy red chillies, (de-seeded if you don't like it too spicy)
½ clove of garlic
½ teaspoon of mineral salt
4 tablespoons of raw agave syrup
1 tablespoon of water

Blend all the ingredients together until you have a beautiful orange-red liquid sauce with broken chilli seeds floating around in it.

Serve your wilted greens with sweet chilli sauce poured over the top.

Keep in the fridge and eat on the day of making.

Salads & Dressings

'Think salad is boring? Then think again!'

If there's one thing I have most days it's a salad. Salad is an important part of any healthy diet. Whether you're aiming to eat more raw, high raw or 100% raw, salad will usually make up part of what you eat every day.

But, let's face it, salad can get quite boring. It's easy to be unimaginative. If you only have one or two salad recipes in your repertoire, it's easy to get stuck in a salad rut. Soon you become bored of eating the same old salad every day and, before you know it, you're on that slippery slope back to eating unhealthy food again.

This is a stumbling block that many people encounter when they first get into raw food. To give yourself the best possible chance of staying on the raw path, it's important that you inspire yourself with a varied selection of raw salad recipes. One of the greatest gifts you can give yourself as a healthy eater is the gift of choice. The recipes in this chapter are here to show you what's actually possible when you get creative with your veg. The diverse colours make them visually exciting, whilst also being full of fresh and exotic flavours.

By experimenting with different flavours, tastes and textures, you'll soon discover that salad doesn't have to be boring and getting enough greens needn't be a chore. Fresh herbs are also leafy greens. They have a high nutritional value and can add an extra dimension to even the simplest of salads. Making sure you have a couple of yummy dressings tucked away in the fridge means that you can whip up a delicious and satisfying salad in moments.

As you become more confident about what's possible with salad, and familiarise yourself with all the different taste combinations, you'll soon find that you intuitively know what works together and what doesn't. Being successful at raw food has a lot to do with learning which raw flavours and textures appeal most to you, and then mixing it up every once in a while by eating something you're totally not expecting. By being willing and open to trying new things you'll find that eating more raw becomes easier and easier.

Mexican Salad

I call this salad Mexican salad because I was thinking of Mexican flavours when I conjured it up. It's got that delicious mix of light and full bodied flavours that mix in your mouth to make magic.

Equipment: knife, chopping board
Serves 1 as a main or 3 as a side dish

2 lettuce leaves, finely shredded
¼ cucumber, diced
10 black olives, pitted
1 tablespoon of coriander leaves, chopped
1 avocado, peeled and diced
1 corn on the cob, de-cobbed

Dressing

½ lime, juice of
3 tablespoons of extra virgin olive oil
¼ teaspoon of chilli powder, or to taste
nutritional yeast flakes, to garnish (optional)

Mix all the ingredients together, except the yeast flakes. Sprinkle the yeast flakes over your salad and serve.

Keep in the fridge and eat on the day of making.

Fennel & Avocado Salad

This is such a deliciously light and elegant salad. It's a great one for serving to non-raw folk, and you can toast the pine nuts if you prefer.

Equipment: knife, chopping board, zester
Serves 1 as a main or 3 as a side dish

2 fennel bulbs, finely sliced
1 small handful of pine nuts
1 avocado, peeled and diced
1 small handful of raisins (optional)

Dressing

3 tablespoons of extra virgin olive oil
½ lemon, juice & zest
1 pinch of mineral salt
1 pinch of black pepper

Mix all your ingredients together and enjoy!

Keep in the fridge and eat on the day of making.

Mango Sea Salad

I created this salad on my 36th birthday because I wanted something a bit special. Since then it's become one of my favourites. Whenever I feel like treating myself, I nip to our fabulous local veg shop and buy one of their always-ripe mangoes so I can whip up this lovely recipe.

Equipment: knife, chopping board, blender (optional)
Serves 1 as a main or 3 as a side dish

3 handfuls of lettuce, shredded
½ yellow or red pepper, de-seeded
2 tomatoes, diced
1 avocado, peeled & diced
1 mango, diced
1 handful of salad seaweed (soaked if necessary) or 3 tablespoons nori sprinkles

Dressing

1 tablespoon of extra virgin olive oil
1 teaspoon cider vinegar
mineral salt, to taste
2 teaspoons of raw sweet chilli sauce (optional – see p.104 for recipe)

Combine all the salad ingredients, pour over the dressing and toss together.

Keep in the fridge and eat on the day of making.

Sunshine Salad

This salad cheers me up every time I make it, and it's the one that gets the most 'wows' when people see it. This salad represents one of my greatest joys with raw food - the colours!

Equipment: knife, chopping board, grater, zester
Serves 1 as a main or 3 as a side dish

¼ butternut squash, peeled and grated
1 carrot, thinly sliced
½ orange or yellow pepper, sliced
1 handful of pumpkin seeds
1 celery stick, finely sliced
1 orange, peeled and cut into pieces

Dressing

1 orange, zest and juice
½ teaspoon of turmeric
1 teaspoon of ground coriander
1 teaspoon of ground cumin
6 tablespoons of extra virgin olive oil
1 teaspoon of honey
1 tablespoon of cider vinegar

Combine all the ingredients and serve in a lovely bowl.

Keeps in the fridge for 24 hours.

Big Salad

This is my favourite everyday salad. I went through a phase of eating a variation of it every weekday lunchtime for about 6 months, because it's great for taking to work. Add whatever extras you fancy to jazz it up.

Equipment: knife, chopping board, grater (optional)
Serves 1 as a main or 3 as a side dish

3 handfuls lettuce, shredded
½ yellow or red pepper, de-seeded
2 tomatoes, chopped
½ avocado, peeled & diced
fresh herbs of your choice (e.g. coriander, basil, thyme)

Optional Extras

fennel, finely sliced
olives, pitted
red cabbage, finely sliced
carrot, grated

Chop the pepper into bite-size pieces and mix together with the lettuce, tomatoes, avocado and herbs.

Add any optional extras and serve with your choice of dressing.

Keep in the fridge and eat on the day of making.

Vietnamese Salad

I love experimenting with the flavours of different cultures. This Vietnamese salad is fresh and sophisticated. Eat it on its own or have it as part of an Asian medley or exciting salad selection.

Equipment: knife, chopping board, peeler
Serves 1 as a main or 3 as a side dish

Dressing

1 clove of garlic
½ small red chilli
2 limes, juiced
1 tablespoon of tamari or nama shoyu
½ teaspoon of honey or raw agave syrup
¼ cup of cashews or sesame seeds
75ml of water to blend

Blend all the dressing ingredients together.

Salad

1 handful of fresh mint leaves, finely chopped
3 handfuls of shredded dark green cabbage or greens
1 handful of fresh coriander leaves, finely chopped
½ cucumber, peeled into ribbons
3 tablespoons of sesame seeds
3 tablespoons of desiccated coconut, raw if possible
1 shallot, finely diced
2 sticks of celery, cut into long fine strips/matchsticks
1 carrot, cut into long fine strips/matchsticks

Combine all the salad ingredients and toss in the dressing.

Keeps in the fridge for 24 hours.

Sesame Coleslaw

I love this coleslaw with baked sweet potato or with my walnut and sage burgers. The sesame gives a lovely rich creaminess without the cloying aspect of mayonnaise that you get in a traditional coleslaw.

Equipment: knife, chopping board, grater
Serves 1 as a main or 3 as a side dish

¼ white cabbage, shredded
2 carrots, grated
1 spring onion
2 dates, pitted

Dressing

2 tablespoons of sesame seeds or tahini
1 tablespoon of lemon juice
4 tablespoons of extra virgin olive oil
1 pinch of mineral salt
½ teaspoon of mustard
½ teaspoon of raw agave syrup

Chop the spring onion and dates finely and mix with the shredded cabbage and grated carrot.

Combine all the dressing ingredients until thoroughly mixed and pour over the salad. Stir the dressing through until the salad is well coated. Leave to marinade for half an hour or eat it straight away.

Keeps in the fridge for 24 hours.

Thai Green Salad

This recipe was inspired by a delicious Thai salad I had at a restaurant. It's fresh and light, and perfect when you feel like an exotic lunch or want an interesting salad to go with supper.

Equipment: knife, chopping board, peeler
Serves 1 as a main or 3 as a side dish

Salad

2 cucumbers or ½ a small green papaya
1 cup of sprouted green lentils or mung beans
2 cups of finely shredded crisp lettuce
3 spring onions, sliced
1 handful of fresh coriander leaves, chopped
1 handful of fresh basil leaves (Thai basil if you can find it), chopped
¼ cup of cashew nuts

Dressing

1 lime, juice of
6 tablespoons of cold pressed sunflower oil
½ large red chilli, finely chopped (and de-seeded if you don't like it too spicy)
½ clove of garlic, crushed or finely chopped
1 tablespoon of tamari or nama shoyu
1 teaspoon of honey or raw agave syrup

Remove the dark green skin from the cucumber or green papaya, then peel the pale flesh into ribbons. Stop peeling when you reach the seeds.

Mix all the dressing ingredients together until they are thoroughly combined.

Toss the salad together with the dressing and serve.

Keep in the fridge and eat on the day of making.

Sprouted Quinoa Salad

If you've ever had tabbouleh you'll love this satisfying salad. The mint and coriander come alive in your mouth. This is also a great recipe when you want a raw substitute for rice.

Equipment: knife, chopping board, sprouting jar or tray
Serves 1 as a main or 3 as a side dish

3 handfuls of sprouted quinoa*
1 handful of fresh parsley, chopped
1 handful of fresh coriander, chopped
1 handful of fresh mint, chopped
2 tomatoes, diced
2 sun dried tomatoes, chopped
1 spring onion

Dressing

½ lemon, juice of
1-2 tablespoons of extra virgin olive oil
1 pinch of mineral salt

Mix all the ingredients together. This salad is great the next day too.

Keeps in the fridge for 24 hours.

* quinoa needs to be very well rinsed 3 times a day during the sprouting process. It takes 2-3 days to sprout.

Spanish Dressing

Add a little flamenco to your salad!

Equipment: knife, chopping board, zester
Makes enough for 2 salads

6 tablespoons of extra virgin olive oil
1 teaspoon of paprika (smoked if possible)
½ teaspoon of ground coriander
¼ orange, zest and juice
1 pinch of mineral salt

Mix all the ingredients together and serve with salads.

Keeps for 5 days in the fridge.

Sun Dried Tomato Dressing

This dressing adds a deep and rich note to any salad.

Equipment: knife, chopping board, blender
Makes enough for 2 salads

6 tablespoons of extra virgin olive oil
3 sun-dried tomato
1 teaspoon of mustard
2 tablespoons of cider vinegar

Blend all the ingredients together and serve with salads.

Keeps for 5 days in the fridge.

Clockwise from top: Spanish Dressing,
Creamy Dressing, Sun Dried Tomato Dressing

Creamy Dressing

This is a richer dressing reminiscent of a traditional mayonnaise.

Equipment: knife, chopping board, blender
Makes enough for 2 salads

6 tablespoons of extra virgin olive oil
1 tablespoon of lemon juice
1 teaspoon of wholegrain mustard
½ teaspoon of honey/raw agave syrup
2 tablespoons of Brazil nuts, macadamia nuts or pine nuts
1 pinch of mineral salt

Blend all the ingredients together and serve with salads.

Keeps for 5 days in the fridge.

Basil Dressing

If you love basil like I do, this is a great way to mix its flavour through your whole salad.

Equipment: knife, chopping board, blender
Makes enough for 2 salads

6 tablespoons of extra virgin olive oil
2 tablespoons of lime juice
1 handful of fresh basil
1 large pinch of mineral salt

Blend all the ingredients together and serve with salads.

Keeps for 5 days in the fridge.

Top Tip: the stalks of the basil are really flavoursome so use them too.

Top: Basil Dressing
Bottom: Japanese Dressing

Japanese Dressing

Equipment: knife, chopping board, blender
Makes enough for 2 salads

6 tablespoons of cold-pressed sunflower oil
1 teaspoon of toasted sesame oil
1 tablespoon of sesame seeds (optional)
1 teaspoon of unpasteurised miso
1cm of fresh ginger
2 tablespoons of rice vinegar
½ teaspoon raw agave syrup or honey

Blend all the ingredients together and serve with salads.

Keeps for 5 days in the fridge.

Top Tip: use a date instead of the raw agave syrup or honey for a richer flavour.

I love oriental flavours, and this dressing hits the spot when I'm looking for something a bit different to jazz up my salad.

Pâtés & Dips

'Eat a rainbow of colours and you'll get a fabulous spectrum of essential nutrients.'

Raw pâtés and dips are great if you are looking to eat more healthily by introducing more raw food into your everyday diet. They're also good for making the transition to eating a high raw diet. When I first started getting into raw food, these recipes were absolute lifesavers. With their rich taste and depth of flavour, they satisfied my cravings for unhealthy comfort foods and helped me to stay on the raw path on many occasions.

Pâtés are very easy to make, so you can easily whip one up at a moment's notice. If your blender isn't of the best quality, just add a little more water to the mixture to make blending easier. Be careful not to add too much too quickly - just add one tablespoon at a time. If you do happen to add a little too much water, don't worry! Just pop it in the fridge and you've got yourself a delicious dressing to drizzle over your next salad.

These recipes are incredibly versatile - my black olive pesto for example, can be spread on cucumber slices, used to stuff mushrooms or tomatoes (a personal favourite), or even used as a pizza topping. There's a huge diversity of flavours you can try and they come in a spectrum of exciting colours. I serve raw pâtés and dips at dinner parties with crudités, eat them as a side dish, or have them as a quick and delicious lunch with veg-sticks, nori wraps, raw crackers or rice cakes.

Because raw pâtés and dips keep in the fridge for up to three days, they're an absolute staple in my house. It's perfect for when you come home feeling hungry after a long day at work, and you're looking for something that's both quick and satisfying. It also works well for kids when they come in famished after school. I like to make a few in advance as they're a big part of my daily diet, so my fridge is usually stocked with a rainbow of pâtés.

Cream 'Cheese'

This raw 'cheese' is the one I use most often. It's super quick and easy, ready in moments for that cheese fix. Spread it on crackers or toast; eat it with crudités.

Equipment: knife, chopping board, blender
Makes enough for 2 servings

1 cup of cashew nuts
1 tablespoon of lemon juice
2 spring onions, pale green part only
2 tablespoons of nutritional yeast (e.g. Engevita)
½ teaspoon of mineral salt
100ml of water

Blend all the ingredients together until smooth. Keeps in the fridge for 24 hours.

'Cheese' Sauce

This sauce is delicious drizzled over salads. I occasionally make dairy-free vegetable bakes with it, and eat it with lightly steamed cauliflower for a dairy-free cauliflower cheese.

Equipment: knife, chopping board, blender
Makes enough for 2 servings

1 cup of cashew nuts
1 tablespoon of lemon juice
2 spring onions, pale green part only
2 tablespoons of nutritional yeast (e.g. Engevita)
1 teaspoon of mineral salt
150ml of water

Blend all the ingredients together until you have a smooth sauce. Keeps in the fridge for 24 hours.

Red Pepper Hummus

This raw hummus is a divine sunset orange colour. I have a particular love of any raw dish that's a more colourful version of its cooked cousin. With raw food you often don't get the heady smells associated with cooked food, so it's great to engage your other senses more. The bright colours of raw food dishes are often what gets people 'oohing and aahing' before they've even tasted it.

Equipment: knife, chopping board, blender
Makes enough for 2 servings

2 red peppers, de-seeded
½ cup of sesame seeds
1 cup of cashews
3 tablespoons of extra virgin olive oil
½ lemon, juice of
1 clove of garlic, crushed
1 teaspoon of mineral salt

Blend all the ingredients together until smooth and creamy.

Keeps in the fridge for 48 hours.

Spicy Walnut Pâté

This pâté is one of my favourites when it's grey and cold outside. The spices give it a delicious depth and warmth of flavour that are exciting no matter what the weather. It's scrumptious with baked potatoes, in salad sandwiches (raw or wheat-free) or as a dip for parties.

Equipment: knife, chopping board, blender
Makes enough for 1 hungry person

1 cup of walnuts, soaked for 8 hours or overnight and then rinsed thoroughly
½ lemon, juice of
2 tablespoons of extra virgin olive oil
¼ teaspoon of mineral salt
1 teaspoon of medium curry powder
¼ teaspoon of paprika
1 clove of garlic
50ml of water

Blend all the ingredients together until smooth and creamy.

Keeps in the fridge for 3 days.

Guacamole

Who doesn't love a good guacamole? When I first started eating raw food this was one of my staples. I stuff mushrooms with it, have it as a simple lunch with rice cakes and salad, or make it for a dip when friends came round. It's so delicious I often eat it by the spoonful!

Equipment: knife, chopping board
Makes enough for 2 servings

2 avocados, peeled and diced
1 small clove of garlic, crushed
1 large pinch of mineral salt
1 pinch of chilli powder
1 lime, juice of
½ red pepper, de-seeded and finely diced
2 tablespoons of fresh coriander, finely chopped
fresh coriander for decorating

In a bowl, mash the avocado with a fork. Stir through the garlic, salt, chilli powder, and lime juice. Stir in the red pepper and fresh coriander. Eat as a dip, spread or with salad.

Best eaten fresh.

Sprouted Green Lentil Hummus

If you're into sprouting, you'll love this recipe. If you're new to sprouting, green lentils are an easy first sprout to grow.   This hummus is delicious with crudités, dehydrated crackers or wrapped in nori sheets with fresh vegetables and a splash of tamari or nama shoyu.

Equipment: knife, chopping board, sprouting jar or tray, blender
Makes enough for 3 servings

2 cups of green lentil sprouts*
1 tablespoon of tahini or sesame seeds
1 clove of garlic, peeled
2 tablespoons of lemon juice
3 tablespoons of extra virgin olive oil
1 pinch of mineral salt

Blend all the ingredients together until smooth.

Keeps in the fridge for 3 days.

*Green lentils need to be soaked overnight, rinsed thoroughly and then sprouted (rinsing two or more times a day) for 3-4 days.

Black Olive Pesto

This deeply flavoursome spread is a bit like tapenade with the added aromatic loveliness of basil. I spread it on cucumber slices, stuff tomatoes with it and use it on raw pizzas.

Equipment: knife, chopping board, blender
Makes enough for 2 servings or 1 pizza

1 cup of good quality pitted black olives
½ clove of garlic, peeled
2 handfuls of basil leaves
3 tablespoons of extra virgin olive oil

Blend all the ingredients together.

Keeps in the fridge for 48 hours.

Beetroot Almond Pâté

The colour of this alone is enough to make my mouth water. It's such a beautiful shade of pink! The rich notes of the cumin offset the earthiness of the beetroot, making this a perfect accompaniment to a cold-day lunch or an evening meal with baked sweet potato and salad.

Equipment: knife, chopping board, blender
Makes enough for 2 servings

½ cup of almonds, soaked overnight, drained and rinsed
1 small beetroot or half a large one, grated
¼ of a lemon, juice of
½ a clove of garlic, peeled
1 tablespoon of nutritional yeast flakes
1 teaspoon of cumin seeds
1 big pinch of mineral salt, or to taste
50ml of water

Blend all the ingredients together to get a smooth pâté consistency.

Keeps in the fridge for 3 days.

Raita

I used to love Indian food (although I find it too rich these days, now that I eat less oily food). Raita always stuck in my mind as something that I wanted to try and reproduce raw. So this is my delicious raw version of the Indian classic.

Equipment: knife, chopping board, blender
Makes enough for 3 servings

½ cup of sunflower seeds, soaked overnight and rinsed
100ml of water
1 tablespoon of lime juice
1 date, pitted
¼ teaspoon of mineral salt
¼ teaspoon of ground black pepper

Blend all the ingredients together until smooth and creamy.

½ cucumber, finely diced
8 mint leaves, chopped finely
1 small handful of coriander leaves, chopped finely

Mix the remaining ingredients through your sunflower seed yoghurt. Garnish with whole mint or coriander leaves.

Keeps in the fridge for 24 hours, although the surface will discolour with time so it's best eaten fresh.

Sun Dried Tomato Pâté

You'd think this pâté would be orange because of the tomato, but it's a lovely olivey green from the fresh coriander. I love tomatoes with any fresh herbs, and coriander works beautifully with the sun dried variety. I spread this pâté on raw crackers or rice cakes and put a layer of refreshing cucumber on top.

Equipment: knife, chopping board, blender
Makes enough for 1 serving

6 pieces of sun dried tomato, soaked or in olive oil
2 handfuls of sunflower seeds, soaked overnight and rinsed
1 spring onion, pale green part only
½ lime, juice of
1 handful of fresh coriander
4 tablespoons of water

Blend all the ingredients together until smooth and pâté-like.

Keeps in the fridge for 48 hours.

Walnut Pesto

There's a brilliant deli in Ashburton, in Devon, that sells a cooked version of this pesto. I loved it so much when I tried it that I went home and created this raw, dairy-free recipe. It's delicious simply scooped up with celery sticks, or stirred through pasta, raw or cooked.

Equipment: knife, chopping board, blender
Makes enough for 1 serving

1 cup of walnuts, soaked for 8 hours or overnight
2 spring onions
2 tablespoons of lemon juice
½ teaspoon of mineral salt
4 tablespoons of nutritional yeast flakes (e.g. Engevita)
50ml of water

Rinse the walnuts until the water runs clear.

Blend all the ingredients until smooth and creamy.

Keeps in the fridge for 48 hours.

Soups

'Raw soups are one of the main staples of my diet in the winter, and I love them in the summer for a quick, light lunch.'

People are often surprised to discover that raw food doesn't have to mean cold food. Soups and sauces can be heated up using a very simple method - just boil the kettle! Warm raw soups are delicious, and perfect for when you're craving some good old fashioned soul food. When it's grey outside, there's nothing quite like a bowl of comforting homemade soup. The trick to making warm soups is to use hot water in your recipe. Heating your bowl will also stop it from sucking the warmth out of your soup. By just adding boiled water to a raw soup, you can whip up a nurturing and sustaining meal packed full of nutrients in a matter of minutes

Because raw soups are super quick to make and easy for the body to digest, they are perfect if you want to eat more healthily but don't have much time to spare. I like to eat them with dehydrated crackers, or wheat free toast and often have one as a light lunch or simple supper. You can also prepare them in advance, so they're ready to take to work with you. If you want to do this, make the recipe at home using only a third of the water specified. When you're ready to eat your soup at work, just boil the kettle and add hot water to create a deliciously warming and healthy lunch.

It goes without saying that raw soups are so much tastier than anything shop-bought. They're also a very easy and affordable way of making sure that you get plenty of nourishing leafy greens in your diet. Among my favourites are spinach soup and pea and mint soup.

Always try and buy fresh ingredients, and use them up within a week. Vegetables tend to lose much of their nutritional value if they're hanging around too long, or when they're frozen. The raw and fresh state of the ingredients will intensify their wonderful tastes and aromatic flavours.

Comforting and hearty, or soothingly sophisticated, when you're craving simplicity or are in a hurry, raw soups are the easiest way to take a few humble ingredients and turn them into a satisfying meal.

Spinach Soup

This is Popeye soup! Its beautiful green colour and delicious creaminess make me happy all year round. Eat it cold in summer or warm in winter, with or without wheat-free toast or raw crackers for a satisfying lunch or light supper.

Equipment: knife, chopping board, blender
Makes 1 large or 2 small bowls of soup

3 handfuls of young spinach
1 avocado, peel and stone removed
1 spring onion, pale part only
1cm of fresh ginger
¾ teaspoon of mineral salt
300ml of warm water (200ml boiling water and 100ml cold water, mixed)

Blend all the ingredients together until smooth.

Best eaten on the day of making, but will last 24 hours in the fridge.

.

Creamy Celery Soup

Celery is so good for us but when I first started eating raw food I struggled with how to get more of it into my diet. In this deliciously creamy soup you get a wonderful hit of celery to rehydrate and alkalise you.

Equipment: knife, chopping board, blender
Makes 1 large or 2 small bowls of soup

5 sticks of celery
½ avocado, peel and stone removed
1 spring onion
¾ teaspoon of mineral salt
300ml of warm water (200ml boiling water and 100ml cold water, mixed)

Blend all the ingredients together until smooth. Decorate with a drizzle of olive oil, a few fine slices of celery and a sprinkle of paprika, if you have it.

Best eaten on the day of making, but will last 24 hours in the fridge.

Dill & Cashew Soup

This is one of my clients' all-time favourites. If you like dill, make the most of its seasonal appearance and create this beautifully flavoured soup for yourself and friends.

Equipment: knife, chopping board, blender
Makes 1 large or 2 small bowls of soup

1 handful of cashews
2 tomatoes
1 handful of fresh dill
¼ of a yellow pepper, de-seeded
1 tablespoon of nama shoyu or tamari
1cm of fresh ginger
1 spring onion
300ml of warm water (200ml boiling water and 100ml cold water, mixed)

Blend all your ingredients together until smooth. Decorate with a drizzle of olive oil and dill fronds.

Best eaten on the day of making, but will last 24 hours in the fridge.

Italian Tomato Soup

I love Italy! I love the flavours of Italy. This soup conjures up the sun and its warmth for me. The olives give it heartiness whilst the tomatoes and spring onion keep it fresh.

Equipment: knife, chopping board, blender
Makes 1 large or 2 small bowls of soup

4 ripe vine tomatoes
½ teaspoon of salt
1 spring onion, the pale green part
1 tablespoon of extra virgin olive oil
5 black olives, pitted
1 tablespoon of dried or 2 tablespoons of fresh oregano
100ml of hot water

Blend all ingredients until smooth.

This soup is best eaten soon after making. If left to stand for long it separates - just stir it with a spoon to mix it back together.

Pea & Mint Soup

I remember serving this special soup on my first ever retreat. Everyone was in raptures! It works brilliantly as a sophisticated starter, or leave out the mint for a winning soup for kids.

Equipment: knife, chopping board, blender
Makes 1 large or 2 small bowls of soup

½ ripe avocado, peel and stone removed
2 handfuls of fresh or defrosted frozen peas
5 mint leaves
1 spring onion, pale green part only
½ teaspoon of mineral salt
300ml of warm water (200ml boiling water and 100ml cold water, mixed)

Blend all these lovely ingredients together until smooth and creamy. Decorate with mint leaves before serving.

Best eaten on the day of making, but will last 24 hours in the fridge.

Thai Soup

If you like a bit of a kick to your food, this warming soup delivers. This is one of my warm winter staples, although I love it cold in the summer too.

Equipment: knife, chopping board, blender
Makes 1 large or 2 small bowls of soup

1 tablespoon fresh Thai red curry paste (see below)
1 courgette, topped and tailed
2 tomatoes
1 celery stick
1-2 teaspoons of tamari or nama shoyu
300ml of warm water (200ml boiling water and 100ml cold water, mixed)
coriander leaves to decorate

Blend all these ingredients until smooth. Put your soup in a bowl and decorate it with coriander leaves.

Best eaten on the day of making, but will last 24 hours in the fridge.

Thai Red Curry Paste

Equipment: knife, chopping board, blender

2.5cm of fresh ginger
2 fresh red chillies
2 kaffir lime leaves, stems removed (soak dried leaves for 30 minutes)
2 spring onions, pale green part only
1 garlic clove, peeled
1 lemon grass, fibrous outer leaves removed
2 big pinches of ground pepper
1 teaspoon of turmeric
4 tablespoons of cold pressed sunflower oil

Blitz everything together until smooth. This paste keeps in the fridge for up to 1 week and is delicious added to dressings, soups and dips.

Pepper & Basil Soup

I love the way raw soups add up to more than the sum of their parts. What seem like quite basic ingredients can combine to create a taste bud explosion that makes you want to close your eyes and just savour the flavour.

Equipment: knife, chopping board, blender
Makes 1 large or 2 small bowls of soup

1½ red, orange or yellow peppers, de-seeded
1 carrot
10 basil leaves
1 spring onion
½ teaspoon of mineral salt
2 tablespoons of extra virgin olive oil
1 tomato
300ml of warm water (200ml boiling water and 100ml cold water, mixed)

Blend all ingredients until smooth. Garnish with basil.

Serve with wheat-free toast and enjoy!

Best eaten on the day of making, but will last 24 hours in the fridge.

Cream of Mushroom Soup

This deliciously creamy soup is a trip down memory lane for me. It reminds me of getting back from long walks to a lovely warm mug of mushroom soup. I think this raw version wins hands down over the cooked version.

Equipment: knife, chopping board, blender
Makes 1 large or 2 small bowls of soup

6 brown mushrooms
1 avocado, peel and stone removed
1 stick of celery
1 tablespoon of tamari or nama shoyu
300ml of warm water (200ml boiling water and 100ml cold water, mixed)

Blend all your ingredients together until creamy and smooth.

Serve drizzled with olive oil.

Best eaten on the day of making, but will last 24 hours in the fridge.

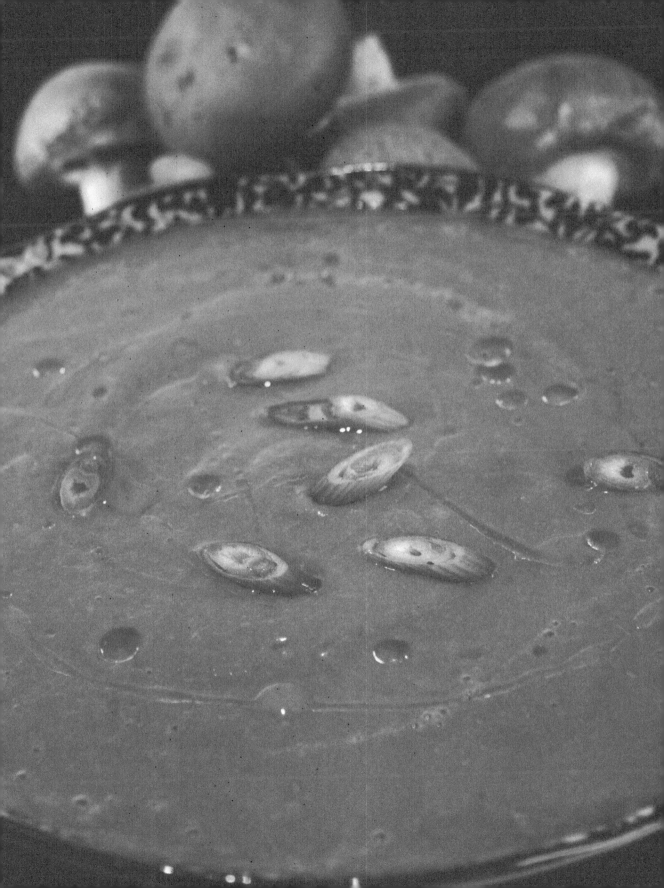

Carrot and Coriander Soup

Carrot and coriander soup is a classic that everyone loves. The raw version is lighter and fresher than its cooked cousin, but it's still an absolute winner when the weather is cold and you want comfort food.

Equipment: knife, chopping board, blender
Makes 1 large or 2 small bowls of soup

3 carrots
½ avocado, peel and stone removed
2 tablespoons of extra virgin olive oil
½ teaspoon of ground coriander
½ teaspoon of ground cumin
½ teaspoon of mineral salt
1cm of fresh ginger
300ml of warm water (200ml boiling water and 100ml cold water, mixed)
1 handful fresh coriander, chopped

Blend all the ingredients together except the fresh coriander. Stir in half the chopped coriander and use the rest to decorate when serving.

Best eaten on the day of making, but will last 24 hours in the fridge.

Fennel Soup

You can get fennel pretty much all year round now. It's such a light and refreshing flavour, and it combines beautifully with the richness of the avocado and the spiciness of the pepper to give you this heart warming soup.

Equipment: knife, chopping board, blender
Makes 1 large or 2 small bowls of soup

1 fennel bulb
½ ripe avocado, peel and stone removed
2 spring onions, pale green part only
1 celery stick
½ lime, juice & zest
½ teaspoon of mineral salt
½ teaspoon of ground black pepper
300ml of warm water (200ml boiling water and 100ml cold water, mixed)

Blend all ingredients together until smooth and creamy.

Best eaten on the day of making, but will last 24 hours in the fridge.

Pasta & Noodles

'Yes, you really can have the perfect comfort food for yourself and the kids in your life. All raw and super healthy!'

Pretty much everyone loves pasta, and I really enjoy watching the look of surprise on people's faces when they discover there's a raw version! Before I discovered raw food, pasta dishes were a huge favourite of mine. Whenever I was craving something warm and comforting, a bowl of pasta was usually the first thing I'd reach for. I used to love how it tasted, but didn't like the way it made me feel afterwards. I'd end up with a post-pasta energy slump and feel like I'd eaten a brick.

I remember how happy I was when I first discovered that there was a raw version of pasta. How exciting! What could it possibly taste like? I couldn't get enough of it when I found out. It meant I could keep eating the food I loved, only now I'd found a version that left me feeling light, refreshed and energised instead of heavy, bloated and sluggish.

I love how easy it is to create such amazingly colourful and delicious dishes that my friends and family enjoy eating as much as I do. Courgettes are one of the best veggies to make raw pasta with. They are a mild vegetable so they absorb all the wonderful flavours of the dish itself, just like regular pasta. You can use a vegetable spiralizer or standard vegetable peeler to make the spaghetti or tagliatelle-like strings, and it's a great way of getting kids more involved in eating raw. They'll love making the spaghetti, and they'll be much more open to trying something new because they've been involved in the preparation. You can mix raw vegetable pasta with wheat-free pasta or noodles too. This gives it that extra touch of warmth and hits the 'cooked' comfort spot, whilst still being a high raw meal.

Courgettes are mostly made up of water, which means that they're very low in calories and a great veggie to opt for if you're trying to lose weight. Other great veggies to make pasta out of include carrots, sweet potato, butternut squash, beetroot and celeriac. Coloured vegetables will affect the colour of your sauce, so if you want a sauce to stay pale stick with pale vegetables. If you're making a tomato pasta sauce, make a rainbow of raw pasta! Whatever your favourite pasta dish, there is a raw alternative.

Cheesy Pasta with Peas

This pasta dish seemed like a mini miracle when I created it. I was craving something comforting and soothing to eat, and this simple combination came to mind. I love peas. I love cheese. I love pasta. But I don't like how cooked pasta and cheese affects me. This recipe hits the pasta comfort spot and gives you energy too.

Equipment: knife, chopping board, blender, peeler/vegetable spiralizer
Makes 1 large bowl or 2 small ones

Cheesy Sauce

1 cup of cashews
2 spring onions
1 tablespoon of lemon juice
2 tablespoons of nutritional yeast flakes (e.g. Engevita)
¾ teaspoon of mineral salt
100ml of water

Blend all ingredients together until smooth and creamy.

2 courgettes, peeled into ribbons or spiralized into 'pasta'
2 cups of shelled fresh peas, or defrosted frozen peas
parsley for garnishing
black pepper

Keep back a handful of peas for garnishing your pasta at the end.

Stir your cheesy sauce through your pasta and peas. Finish with the extra handful of peas, chopped parsley and black pepper.

Best eaten fresh, but will keep in the fridge for 24 hours.

Crossover meal cooked additions: wheat-free spaghetti/rice noodles/boiled egg/ chicken/bacon.

Pasta with Rich Tomato Sauce

I was staying at my Dad's old house in Spain when this recipe came into fruition. It's a perfect lunchtime dish to share with friends or a lovely, satisfying supper.

Equipment: knife, chopping board, blender, peeler/vegetable spiralizer
Makes 1 large bowl or 2 small bowls

Sauce

4 sun dried tomatoes, in oil or soaked
2 fresh tomatoes
1 spring onion, pale green part only
½ cm of fresh ginger
¼ teaspoon of chilli powder (optional)
1 date, pitted
½ lime, juice of
1 tablespoon of extra virgin olive oil
50ml of water

Blend all your sauce ingredients together until smooth.

2 courgettes, with green skin removed
3 tablespoons of extra virgin olive oil
15 olives, pitted and halved
1 handful of pine nuts
1 handful of fresh thyme or basil

Peel the pale flesh of the courgettes into ribbons, or make into 'spaghetti' using a vegetable spiralizer. Mix the courgette ribbons with your tomato sauce and the olives. Serve scattered with the pine nuts and herbs before serving.

Best eaten fresh, but will keep in the fridge for 24 hours.

Crossover meal cooked additions: wheat-free spaghetti/rice noodles/ feta/ bacon.

Pasta Aglio, Olio e Peperoncino

Otherwise known as pasta with garlic, oil and chilli, this is one of my favourite classic Italian pasta dishes – so simple and yet so satisfying.

Equipment: knife, chopping board, peeler/vegetable spiralizer
Makes 1 large bowl or 2 small ones

2 courgettes, green skin removed
½ a clove of garlic
½ a large fresh red chilli
3 tablespoons of extra virgin olive oil
1/3 teaspoon of mineral salt
1 handful of fresh parsley, finely chopped

Peel or spiralize the courgettes for your pasta.

Finely chop your chilli, removing the seeds beforehand if you don't like your food too spicy. In a mixing bowl, add all your ingredients together and combine thoroughly. Serve up and finish with a final drizzle of olive oil.

Best eaten fresh, but will keep in the fridge for 24 hours.

Crossover meal cooked additions: wheat-free spaghetti/rice noodles/tofu/bacon.

Italian Veg Pasta

The colours in this recipe are gorgeous. This dish gets better with some time, allowing the flavours to merge and make magic together. You can make a double portion and have some for lunch tomorrow too.

Equipment: knife, chopping board, peeler/vegetable spiralizer
Serves 1 -2, depending on how hungry you are

2 courgettes, spiralized or peeled into pasta
½ red pepper, diced
2 tomatoes, diced
1 handful of pitted olives, chopped
1 handful of red cabbage, diced
1 tablespoon of dried oregano or 2 tablespoons of fresh oregano
1 tablespoon of cider vinegar
1 tablespoon of nama shoyu or ½ teaspoon mineral salt
3 tablespoons of extra virgin olive oil

Mix all the ingredients together. You can leave the mixture to marinade for a while or eat it straight away. Best eaten fresh, but will keep in the fridge for 24 hours.

Crossover meal cooked additions: wheat-free pasta/tofu/feta/pancetta.

Pesto & Pasta

Pesto pasta, raw styley! Forget the post-supper energy slump with this dish. Kids love it. Adults can't believe how good it is. This pesto recipe is a traditional pesto, minus the parmesan.

Equipment: knife, chopping board, blender, peeler/vegetable spiralizer
Makes 1 large bowl or 2 smaller bowls

2 courgettes, peeled into ribbons or spiralized for 'pasta'
1 handful of pine nuts
1 handful of fresh basil
1 clove of garlic, peeled (optional)
1 tablespoon of nutritional yeast flakes (optional)
½ teaspoon of mineral salt
4 tablespoons of extra virgin olive oil
2 teaspoons of lemon juice
1 tablespoon of water
basil to garnish

To make the pesto, blend all the ingredients together until smooth. According to your personal taste, add more nuts for a deeper/creamier flavour, more oil for an oilier texture, more basil for a stronger flavour, or more water if it's too rich.

Pour onto your 'pasta' and toss well for even coverage, then serve topped with more fresh basil!

Best eaten fresh, but will keep in the fridge for 24 hours.

Crossover meal cooked additions: wheat-free spaghetti/tofu/goat's cheese/ chicken pieces.

Macaroni Cheese

I make up a batch of the yummy topping and freeze it. You can use it like parmesan to top all kinds of dishes.

Equipment: knife, chopping board, blender, coffee grinder or mini food processor (optional)
Serves 2

Cheesy Topping

50g Brazil nuts, finely chopped or processed
1 tablespoon of nutritional yeast flakes (e.g. Engevita)
1 clove of garlic, crushed
¼ teaspoon of mineral salt
1 teaspoon of lemon juice
¼ teaspoon of smoked paprika

Mix all your topping ingredients together.

2 courgettes, peeled and cut into 'pasta' rectangles ½ cm by 3cm

Sauce

1 cup of cashews
2 spring onions
1 tablespoon of lemon juice
2 tablespoons of nutritional yeast flakes (e.g. Engevita)
¾ teaspoon of mineral salt
1 big pinch of ground turmeric (optional)
150ml of water

Blend all the sauce ingredients until smooth and creamy. Pour over your courgette pasta and mix thoroughly. Put your macaroni in a serving bowl and finish with your cheesy topping.

Best eaten fresh, but will keep in the fridge for 24 hours.

Crossover meal cooked additions: wheat-free pasta/ham.

Three Mushroom Pasta

This soothing creamy pasta recipe is one of my favourites. I'm a great fan of mushrooms, in all their forms. I particularly love porcini mushrooms with this dish.

Equipment: knife, chopping board, blender, peeler/vegetable spiralizer
Serves 1

2 courgettes, green skin removed

Creamy Sauce

1 cup of cashews
¾ teaspoon of mineral salt
100ml of water
black pepper

Choose 3 types of mushroom from this list:

2 chestnut mushrooms, sliced
2 oyster mushrooms, sliced
4 button mushrooms, quartered
6 pieces of dried porcini mushroom, rehydrated in water and rinsed
3 wild mushrooms, sliced

fresh thyme (optional)

Blend all your creamy sauce ingredients until smooth.

Peel or spiralize your courgette into pasta and stir the sauce and mushrooms through. Top with a drizzle of olive oil and some fresh thyme if you have it.

Best eaten fresh, but will keep in the fridge for 24 hours.

Crossover meal cooked additions: wheat-free pasta/tofu/chicken pieces.

Japanese Noodles

I love the oriental flavours of this dish. It's so easy to make - just a matter of chopping, peeling and mixing, so it couldn't be simpler.

Equipment: knife, chopping board, peeler/vegetable spiralizer
Serves 1 – 2, depending on how hungry you are

2 courgettes, peeled into ribbons or spiralized for noodles
8 cherry tomatoes/2 tomatoes, chopped
1 handful of baby spinach, shredded
1 spring onion, pale green part only, finely sliced
5cm of cucumber, cut into matchsticks
¼ cup of salad seaweed (soaked if necessary)
1 tablespoon of chopped coriander leaves

Dressing

1cm of fresh ginger, finely chopped
3 tablespoons of cold pressed sunflower oil
½ red chilli, seeds removed and finely chopped
½ teaspoon of toasted sesame oil (optional)
2 teaspoons of cider vinegar
1 teaspoon of raw agave syrup
2 teaspoons of tamari or nama shoyu

Toss all the ingredients together until thoroughly combined.

Best eaten fresh, but will keep in the fridge for 24 hours.

Crossover meal cooked additions: wheat-free or buckwheat noodles/tofu/ salmon pieces.

Thai Noodles

Since I shared this recipe with my sister she feeds it to all her friends to get them interested and excited about raw food. It's so tasty that it works every time!

Equipment: knife, chopping board, blender, peeler/vegetable spiralizer, zester
Serves 1

3 courgettes with green skin removed, or 4 carrots
1 stick of lemon grass, peeled back to the soft part
½ lime, juice & zest
2 dates, pitted
1 tablespoon of nama shoyu or tamari
1cm of fresh ginger
½ clove of garlic, peeled
1 handful of cashew nuts
½ teaspoon of dried red chilli flakes (optional)
100ml of water

To Decorate

1 spring onion, pale green part, sliced at an angle for decoration
1 tablespoon of fresh coriander, finely chopped

Peel the courgettes or carrots (or a mix of both) into ribbons, or turn into 'noodles' with a vegetable spiralizer.

Blend the lemon grass, lime zest, dates, nama shoyu or tamari, ginger, garlic, cashews and chilli together with the water to make a syrupy sauce. Stir your sauce through the 'noodles'. Serve topped with fresh coriander and thin diagonal slices of spring onion.

Best eaten fresh, but will keep in the fridge for 24 hours.

Crossover meal cooked additions: wheat-free or rice noodles/tofu/chicken pieces.

Veggie Noodles

These noodles have a Chinese flavour, so if you love Chinese food but want to give up the greasiness of a take-away this is a deliciously healthy alternative.

Equipment: knife, chopping board, mandolin (optional)
Serves 1

Sauce

1 tablespoon of tamari or nama shoyu
½ lime, juice of
1 small garlic clove, crushed
1cm of fresh ginger, finely chopped
1 small red chilli, chopped (optional)
3 tablespoons of cold pressed vegetable oil

Vegetables

½ red onion, finely sliced
100g shiitake mushrooms, finely sliced
½ red pepper, finely chopped
4 asparagus spears, sliced
1 tablespoon of chopped fresh coriander

Noodles

2 courgettes
1 teaspoon of chopped fresh coriander, to garnish

For the noodles, finely slice the courgettes along their length (or use a mandolin if you have one). Then cut each slice into 1cm wide long strips to make ribbon noodles.

Mix your sauce, vegetables and courgette noodles together.

Best eaten fresh, but will keep in the fridge for 24 hours.

Crossover meal cooked additions: wheat-free or buckwheat noodles/tofu/pork

Main Meals

'The evening meal is often the most challenging meal of the day when you 'go raw'. Once you have the right recipes all that changes, especially knowing that you can add in a few cooked elements if you want to.'

Out of all the raw food workshops I run, my workshop on raw food main meals is one of the most popular. The people who come are there either because they're interested in embracing the raw food lifestyle, or are simply looking to eat more healthily. They are bored of eating salad and need inspiration to keep them on the healthy-eating path. When people first discover raw food it's quite normal for them to doubt their willpower as they wave goodbye to the cooked foods they know and love.

I encourage you to focus on finding raw food dishes you love, and on opening your mind to the delicious and satisfying main meals that are possible. Eating raw makes you think outside the box and exposes a whole world of tastes and flavours that you didn't even know existed. It gives you the opportunity to sample exotic ingredients and experiment with new and exciting taste combinations. People usually find that within a couple of weeks of eating raw they barely think about the cooked comfort foods they used to love, because they've found such a deliciously healthy alternative in raw food.

It's important to make sure you don't get locked into eating the same raw recipes each day, however delicious they might be. If you make your meals diverse and interesting, you'll find that it's far easier to stay eating healthily. Choose recipes that interest and excite you, and remember that variety is key. By keeping your taste buds on their toes, you'll find that it's much easier to stay passionate and inspired about raw food.

When you're craving the cooked food factor, you can also make your meals 'half and half'. This is when you add cooked elements to a dish to make it 'high raw' rather than all raw. I tend to add brown rice, wheat-free spaghetti or a baked sweet potato. Alternatively, you can add cooked protein in the form of tofu, eggs, fish or meat. This is great for when you're eating with family or friends, because it means that you don't have to make one meal for yourself and a different one for everyone else. Plus, it also makes it more appealing to people who might not be into raw food. Most of all, I encourage you to have fun exploring and trying out different recipes. Happy adventures with your main meals!

Satay Veg

This is a dish I often take round to friends' houses. It's a great party dish because everyone loves it, whether they know about raw food or not. It's delicious!

Equipment: knife, chopping board, blender
Serves 1

Satay Sauce

¼ cup of cashews
½ clove of garlic, peeled
¼ teaspoon of chilli flakes (optional)
1 teaspoon of honey/raw agave syrup
1 tablespoon of tamari or nama shoyu
2 tablespoons of extra virgin coconut oil
70ml of water
1 tablespoon of lime juice

Blend all these ingredients until smooth and creamy.

Vegetables

½ yellow pepper
½ courgette
1 portobello mushroom, stem removed
6 tablespoons of extra virgin olive oil
1 small handful of cashews

Cut the vegetables into 2.5cm squares and toss them in the satay sauce. Scatter with the whole cashews and serve on a bed of salad or with brown rice.

Best eaten fresh, but will keep in the fridge for 24 hours.

Crossover meal cooked additions: brown rice/baked potato/tofu/prawns/chicken pieces.

Walnut & Sage Burgers

These burgers are deeply satisfying. I like to eat them with a big salad and the rich tomato sauce overleaf. If you've got a dehydrator it's nice to dehydrate them for 2-4 hours. If you don't have a dehydrator, eat them as they are or put them in the oven on the lowest heat, with the door slightly ajar, to heat through for a few hours.

Equipment: knife, chopping board, food processor, blender
Makes 6 small burgers or 3 large ones

50g raw buckwheat, soaked for 60 minutes or more
100g walnuts
1 celery stick
2 spring onions, pale green parts only
2 medium sized carrots, grated
½ teaspoon of ground coriander
½ teaspoon of ground cumin
5 fresh sage leaves
½ teaspoon of mineral salt
50g poppy seeds (optional, for coating the burgers)
4 sage leaves, finely chopped (optional, for coating the burgers)

Set aside the poppy seeds and sage leaves for the final burger coating, if you're using them.

Process the remaining ingredients in a food processor until the mixture is finely processed.

Mould the mixture into 3 large or 6 small burger shapes. Roll the burgers in the poppy seeds or finely chopped sage leaves (or a mixture of both). Serve with the rich tomato sauce on the next page, and salad.

Best eaten fresh, but will keep in the fridge for 24 hours.

Crossover meal cooked additions: steamed veg/boiled or new potatoes.

Rich Tomato Sauce

Equipment: knife, chopping board, blender
Makes enough for 2 servings

4 sun dried tomatoes
2 fresh tomatoes
1 spring onion, pale green part only
½ cm of fresh ginger
1 pinch of chilli powder (optional)
1 date, pitted
½ lime, juice of
1 tablespoon of extra virgin olive oil
50ml of water

Blend all the ingredients until smooth and serve this sauce as a relish.

Best eaten fresh, but will keep in the fridge for 24 hours.

This deliciously rich tomato sauce is the perfect balance to any nut-based burgers, patties, falafels and loaves. I love it best with my walnut and sage burgers.

Nori Wraps

This is so super simple – as long as you have nori sheets (seaweed sheets used for sushi) in your cupboard, you've always got a delicious meal that's just seconds away from eating. This is a super easy raw equivalent of the sandwich.

Equipment: knife, chopping board, none
Serves 1

2 nori seaweed sheets (preferably untoasted)

Your choice of the following:
raw pâté
wasabi paste
finely sliced fresh ginger
avocado
lettuce
tomato
cucumber
sprouted seeds
celery
mushrooms
seeds
peppers
sun dried tomatoes
nama shoyu or tamari
or whatever else you fancy

Place your chosen ingredients on a nori sheet and wrap.

Don't hang around. Eat it now!

Crossover meal cooked additions: tofu/egg/salmon

Broccoli & Mushroom Stir

A lot of people haven't tried broccoli raw. It's delicious! If you're adding it to a recipe, I find the trick is to cut it up small. It makes it easier to chew and digest. Having said that, I'll quite happily dunk large florets into raw pâtés and hummus too.

Equipment: knife, chopping board, zester
Serves 1 – 2, depending on how hungry you are

2 cups of broccoli, cut into very small florets
½ cup of leek, finely shredded
8 button mushrooms, quartered
1 stick of celery, finely sliced
14 green olives, pitted and halved
8 basil leaves, bruised and shredded
2 tablespoons of extra virgin olive oil
½ red chilli, de-seeded and finely chopped
1cm of fresh ginger, finely chopped
½ clove of garlic, peeled and finely chopped
½ lemon, zest and juice
1 big pinch of mineral salt
1 big pinch of ground black pepper

Combine all the ingredients together, massaging the veg between your fingers to soften a little. Allow to marinade for a minimum of 1 hour or overnight.

This recipe is also delicious heated in a dehydrator for 2 hours.

Keeps in the fridge for 24 hours.

Crossover meal cooked additions: rice/rice noodles/tofu/halloumi cheese/ chicken pieces.

Vegetable Cheese Tarts

These are such beautiful looking little tarts. Despite the number of ingredients it's surprisingly fun and quick to make for something that looks so impressive. I like to serve them at special occasions with a medley of exciting salads.

Equipment: knife, chopping board, food processor, blender, chefs rings* (see next page)
Serves 4

Crust

150g almonds
1 ½ carrots, grated
1 tablespoon of extra virgin coconut oil
1 handful of fresh basil

Process the crust ingredients together in a food processor until finely chopped. Put your chefs rings on a flat, movable surface such as a plate. Divide the crust mixture between your four moulds, pressing into the bottom and up the sides to create the crust. Put them in the fridge while you make the next bits.

Filling

200g cashew nuts
2 tablespoons of nutritional yeast flakes (e.g. Engevita)
2 spring onions, white parts only
2 tablespoons of lemon juice
¾ teaspoon of mineral salt
120ml of water

¼ cup of chopped chives

Combine all the filling ingredients, except the chopped chives, in a blender until smooth. Stir in the chopped chives. With your crusts still in their moulds, pour the filling into them and spread out evenly with a spatula or knife. Put your tarts back in the fridge.

Continued on next page ...

Topping

½ red pepper, de-seeded and cut into strips
3 baby asparagus, tender parts only (optional)
1 small handful of rocket
2 tablespoons of extra virgin olive oil
1 teaspoon of lemon juice

Mix the pepper, rocket and baby asparagus in with the olive oil, lemon juice and salt. Allow to marinade for ½ an hour.

To Finish

1. Take your tarts out of the fridge.

2. Run a knife around the edge of the chefs rings, cutting the crust away from the edge.**

3. Whilst still in their moulds, place the tarts on the plate(s) you're going to serve them on.

4. Remove the chefs rings.

5. Decorate each tart with the vegetable topping.

For a simple meal serve with salad, or go all out with the accompaniments if you're making them for a dinner party.

Best eaten fresh, but will keep in the fridge for 24 hours.

* If you don't have chefs ring, you can use tartlet tins or an 18cm cake tin to make one big tart. Line your tartlet tins or cake tin with a piece of cling film that's too big. You will then be able to pull your tarts out of their moulds later.

** If you lined your tartlet or cake tin with cling film, use the cling film to remove your tarts from their moulds.

Crossover meal cooked additions: steamed veg.

This is my favourite dinner party dish. It tastes so good that everyone loves it, raw or not. I get to eat the food I love and share it with the people I love!

Guacamole Mushrooms

This is the recipe that I mentioned in the pâtés and dips chapter. It never fails to satisfy. I eat it simply with salad.

Equipment: knife, chopping board
Serves 1 – 2, depending on how hungry you are

2 portobello mushrooms, stems removed
3 tablespoons of extra virgin olive oil
1 teaspoon of tamari or nama shoyu
1 tablespoon of lime juice

Marinade the mushrooms in the oil, tamari and lime juice for 20 minutes, making sure the mushrooms are fully coated in marinade and turning from time to time.

2 avocados, peel and stone removed
½ red pepper, de-seeded and finely diced
1 small clove of garlic, crushed
1 large pinch of mineral salt
1 pinch of chilli powder
1 lime, juice of
2 tablespoons of fresh coriander, finely chopped
fresh coriander for decorating

Mash the avocado with a fork, adding in the garlic, salt, chilli powder, and lime juice. Stir in the red pepper and fresh coriander.

Drain the marinade from the mushrooms.

Pile the guacamole onto the mushrooms and top with a few coriander leaves.

Best eaten fresh, but will keep in the fridge for 24 hours.

Crossover meal cooked additions: brown rice/chicken.

Raw Stir Fry

This favourite of mine combines the aromatic flavour of lime with ginger and garlic to give a fresh zinginess that I love all year round. In the summer I eat it on its own, and in the winter I eat it with a baked sweet potato.

Equipment: knife, chopping board, zester
Serves 1 – 2, depending on how hungry you are

1 pak choi or 1 handful of spinach
½ red, yellow or orange pepper
5 baby corn, or ½ corn on the cob
4 mushrooms
10 mange tout or sugar snap peas

Finely slice the pak choi or spinach along the long length of the leaves. Finely slice the pepper into strips. Cut the baby corn into quarters, length ways, or de-cob the corn with a sharp knife. Slice the mushrooms. Cut the mange tout or sugar snap peas in half.

Sauce

½ red chilli, de-seeded (optional)
1cm of fresh ginger
½ clove of garlic
1 lime, zest and juice
1 tablespoon of fresh coriander, chopped
3 tablespoons of nama shoyu or tamari

Finely chop the chilli, if using. Finely chop the ginger with the garlic. Mix together with the lime zest and juice, coriander and nama shoyu or tamari. Add to your chopped veggies and allow to marinate for at least 10 minutes.

Keeps in the fridge for 24 hours.

Crossover meal cooked additions: brown rice/rice noodles/baked sweet potato/ tofu/prawns/chicken.

Stuffed Peppers

These stuffed peppers are great if you've got some left-over pâté or dip that you want to use up. They are good for taking to work, or for serving up at dinner parties because they look so pretty.

Equipment: knife, chopping board, blender
Serves 1 – 2, depending on how hungry you are

1 red, orange or yellow pepper
raw pâté of your choice, such as sunflower pâté, cream 'cheese' or guacamole
fresh herbs to decorate

Slice your pepper in half and de-seed it. You may want to leave the stalks on for decoration. Alternatively, you can cut the top off the whole pepper, creating a red pepper 'bowl'.

Take your pâté and spoon the mixture into your pepper. Top with a sprinkling of fresh herbs and serve with salad.

Keeps in the fridge for 24 hours.

Crossover meal cooked additions: feta cheese/boiled potatoes or new potatoes/ steamed veg.

Ratatouille

Ratatouille used to be one of my favourite cooked dishes. This raw version is absolutely delicious with brown rice or a baked potato.

Equipment: knife, chopping board, blender
Serves 1 – 2, depending on how hungry you are

½ a courgette
¼ of an aubergine (optional)
4 mushrooms
½ a red pepper
10 black olives
4 tomatoes
1 tablespoon of oregano
2 tablespoons of extra virgin olive oil
1 tablespoon of lemon juice
½ date, pitted
2.5cm of fresh ginger
1 teaspoon of mineral salt
1 spring onion

Blend three of the tomatoes with the oregano, olive oil, lemon juice, date, ginger, salt and spring onion.

Chop the rest of the veg into 1cm pieces and marinade in the sauce for at least ½ an hour or overnight.

Keeps in the fridge for 24 hours.

Crossover meal cooked additions: baked potato/brown rice/tofu/feta/minced beef.

Thai Red Curry

Just because you eat raw doesn't mean you have to give up curry! This Thai red curry gives new meaning and new life to the concept of curry.

Equipment: knife, chopping board, grater
Serves 2

Veg

200g butternut squash, peeled and finely grated
1 red pepper, cut into small pieces
3 mushrooms, cut into small pieces
2 tomatoes, cut into small pieces
1 courgette, cut into small pieces
½ avocado, peeled and cut into small pieces
coriander leaves, to decorate

Curry Sauce

2 tablespoons of Thai red curry paste (see p.172)
2 tablespoons of lime juice
250ml of coconut milk
2 tablespoons of nama shoyu or tamari
150ml of hot water

Stir all the sauce ingredients together until well mixed

Combine your prepared veg with your curry sauce. Top with coriander leaves and serve.

Keeps in the fridge for 24 hours.

Crossover meal cooked additions: brown rice/rice noodles/tofu/prawns/white fish/chicken pieces.

Desserts

'Thank Mother Nature for raw pudding!'

Raw desserts and puddings are my favourite bit about discovering raw food. I've always been a real foodie and loved preparing deliciously indulgent desserts and puddings for myself, my friends and my family. Before I began my raw food journey, I worried that eating this healthily would mean I'd have to wave goodbye to dishes that I'd loved since childhood and be left with nothing exciting to look forward to on the sweet front. How wrong I was!

I was so amazed when I discovered that there was even such a thing as a raw cheesecake. I remember the first time I ever tried one, I couldn't quite believe how good it tasted! I remember thinking 'who would have thought that pudding could be this delicious AND healthy?' I'd discovered the ultimate guilt-free pleasure.

Raw puddings are as sophisticated, indulgent and as diverse as cooked puddings but, because they're free of the refined flour, sugar, butter and cream of traditional desserts, you'll find that they won't leave you feeling weighed down or putting on weight. Traditional desserts tend to taste great when we're actually eating them, and we might even feel a temporary boost in our energy levels or mood (known as a 'sugar high'), but this short-term boost inevitably leads to a sugar crash, and we're left feeling lethargic, moody and bloated.

The brilliant thing about raw desserts is that when

you are in need of comfort food, you can have a raw pudding and feel absolutely great about it. They are fresh and deeply satisfying. I love that I can indulge in a deliciously decadent dessert whenever I like, whilst knowing that I'm still making fabulously healthy choices.

Raw desserts are also the best way to convert people to the idea of raw food. One of the main stumbling blocks that people face is the idea that eating healthily means that you're somehow depriving yourself of something. When people taste a raw dessert for the first time, they soon realise that this couldn't be further from the truth. I've lost count of the amount of people who have opened their minds to raw food after tasting raw chocolate mousse, or a delicious raw cheesecake. Because, let's face it, no one can resist a good pudding!

I hope you have as much fun exploring and experimenting with these recipes as I did creating them!

Raspberry Cardamom Chia Pudding

Cardamom is one of my favourite spices and it gives this unpretentious and utterly delicious pudding the delicate kiss of the exotic. I love the tangy contrast and beautiful colour of the pink raspberry puree.

Equipment: blender, muslin/nut milk bag, sieve
Serves 2

Cardamom Milk

1/3 cup of almonds (preferably soaked for 8 hours or overnight, and then rinsed)
200ml of water
1 cardamom pod
2 dates, pitted

Blend all your cardamom milk ingredients together thoroughly. Strain the milk using a jelly bag, muslin or fine sieve.

Pudding

200ml of cardamom milk
3 tablespoons of chia seeds
¼ teaspoon of vanilla essence
1 handful of raspberries, puréed and sieved
raspberries for decorating

In a mixing bowl stir together the chia seeds, cardamom milk and vanilla essence. Soak for an hour, stirring regularly to stop the chia seeds sticking to the bottom of the bowl.

Pour the mixture into pretty serving glasses and leave to set for at least 2 hours or overnight in the fridge. Once your chia puddings have set, pour on the raspberry puree and add a few fresh raspberries on top.

This pudding keeps for 48 hours in the fridge.

Pear Crumble Cup

The light fruitiness of the pear combines beautifully with the richness of the crumble and creamy tartness of the crème fresh. You can have this as a weekend breakfast treat, or jazz it up for a dinner party by serving it in pretty glasses.

Equipment: knife, chopping board, blender
Makes 2 servings

Crumble

½ cup of almonds
¼ cup of pecans
1 date, pitted

In a food processor, process the nuts and date until finely crumbed. Put aside a little crumble, for lightly sprinkling on top at the end.

Crème Fresh

½ cup of cashew nuts
1/3 cup of water
1 teaspoon of nutritional yeast flakes
½ lemon, juice and zest
½ teaspoon of vanilla essence

Blend all the ingredients together until smooth and creamy.

2 pears, peeled and cored

Cut the pears into bite size pieces.

In 2 glasses, layer the pear, crumble and crème fresh in alternate layers, finishing with the crème fresh. Decorate with a light sprinkling of crumble and chill.

Keeps for 24 hours in the fridge.

Fig & Strawberry Crumble

Crumble is not something that one normally associates with summer, but the raw version is perfect for when the weather is warm. Summer fruit crumbles are among my favourites.

Equipment: knife, chopping board, food processor, blender
Serves 4

6 ripe fresh figs
½ teaspoon of vanilla essence
10 strawberries, cut into quarters

Blend 3 of the figs with the vanilla essence until pureed.

Finely chop the remaining 3 figs and mix with the strawberries, leaving a few aside for decoration at the end. Stir through the fig puree and spoon the mixture into a crumble dish.

Crumble

¾ cup of almonds
¼ cup of pecans
1 date, pitted
1 teaspoon of raw agave syrup or honey
2 tablespoons of extra virgin coconut oil

In a food processor, process the nuts and dates. When finely crumbed, add the raw agave syrup or honey and the coconut oil.

Layer the crumble over the fruit mixture so that it covers it evenly. Top with a few strawberries and serve. It's also delicious with the crème fresh on p.240.

Keeps for 48 hours in the fridge.

Lime & Kiwi Cheesecake

If you've never tried raw cheesecake then you're not going to believe how good it is! This lime and kiwi cheesecake takes advantage of the green colour of the avocado to make a low-nut version of the more classic raw cheesecake made with cashews.

Equipment: knife, chopping board, food processor, blender, cake tin, zester
Serves 8

Crust

1 cup of freshly ground almonds
2 pinches of mineral salt
½ cup of medjool dates, pitted

Sprinkle a fine layer of ground almonds over the base of a loose bottomed cake tin (a 20cm tin is a good size for this recipe), or line your cake tin with a big piece of cling film so you can lift the cheesecake out at the end.

Process the ground almonds, salt and medjool dates together until the dates are completely chopped.

With wet hands, press the mixture onto the base and up the sides of your cake tin, until you have your cheesecake pastry case. When the mixture sticks to your fingers, re-wet them before continuing.

Continued on next page...

Filling

3 ripe avocados, peel and stone removed
6 tablespoons of raw agave syrup
120ml of water
1½ limes, zest of
6 tablespoons of lime juice
1 teaspoon of nutritional yeast flakes
1 pinch of mineral salt
¾ cup of extra virgin coconut oil

Melt the coconut oil over a bowl of hot water (see bain-marie instructions on p.278).

Cut the avocados in half and remove the stones. Remove the flesh and put it into a blender with all the other ingredients. Blend until smooth and creamy. Fill your pastry case evenly with this mixture and put your cheesecake-so-far in the freezer for a few hours, to set.

To Decorate

3 kiwis, peeled and thinly sliced

Before serving, decorate your cheesecake with thin slices of peeled kiwi.

This cheesecake keeps in the fridge for 24 hours, although it's best eaten soon after decorating with the kiwis. Alternatively, you can freeze the cheesecake before decorating with the kiwi. When you're ready to eat it, defrost for at least 4 hours and then decorate with fresh kiwis before serving.

"This is delicious! What's in it? ... You mean it's actually good for me? That's fantastic."

A common response when non-raw foodies try this lime & kiwi cheesecake for the first time.

Raspberry Cheesecakes

Don't you just love how these look? I make them using chefs rings (you can buy them in any good kitchen shop or online) but you can use mini-tart tins or a muffin tin instead. Just remember to line them with cling film so you can get your cheesecakes out when they are done.

Equipment: food processor, blender, chefs rings or small cake tins
Makes 2 mini cheesecakes

Crust

½ cup of freshly ground almonds
1 big pinch of mineral salt
¼ cup of medjool dates, pitted

Mix the ground almonds and salt together. Sprinkle a fine layer over the bottom of your chefs rings or mini cake tins.

Process the remaining ground almonds, salt and medjool dates together until the dates are completely chopped. Divide the mixture between your 2 chefs rings or cake tins.

With wet hands, press the mixture into the base and up the sides until you have your cheesecake pastry case. When the mixture sticks to your fingers, re-wet them before continuing.

Continued on next page ...

Filling

¾ cup of cashew nuts
2 teaspoons of lemon zest (about 1 lemon)
2 tablespoons of lemon juice
2 tablespoons of extra virgin coconut oil, melted
3 tablespoons of water
1 tablespoon of vanilla essence or seeds from 2 vanilla beans
½ teaspoon of nutritional yeast flakes

Blend all the ingredients together until smooth and creamy. Fill your crust cases evenly with this mixture and place in the fridge to set.

Topping

100g raspberries
2 tablespoons of raw agave syrup
½ teaspoon of balsamic vinegar
3 tablespoons of extra virgin coconut oil, melted

raspberries to decorate

Blend all the topping ingredients together and pour over your cheesecakes. Arrange your decorative raspberries prettily on top. Put the cheesecakes in the fridge to set for at least 2 hours.

Just before serving, remove your cheesecakes from their moulds and plate up.

Keep in the fridge for up to 3 days. Freezes well without the fresh raspberries on top.

You can use any berry instead of the raspberries in this recipe. Try blueberries for a beautiful lavender coloured cheesecake, or strawberries of extra summer fruitiness.

Mint Chocolate Torte

This is Mark's favourite. When you try it you'll see why.

Equipment: food processor, blender, cake tin, bain-marie (see p.278)
Serves 12 (or cut your cake into slices and keep in the freezer for afternoon treats)

Torte

400g Brazil nuts, ground
100g raw cacao powder
½ cup of raw agave syrup
2 teaspoons of vanilla essence
30g raw cacao butter (or extra virgin coconut oil if you can't get hold of it)

Melt the raw cacao butter using your bain-marie (you can grate it to help it melt quicker).

Grease your cake tin (use a 15-20cm tin) with a little of the melted raw cacao butter. It will go hard as it cools, but that's okay.

Process all the torte ingredients in a food processor, or mix them together by hand in a bowl.

Press the mixture evenly into your cake tin.

Mint Cream

200g cashews
5 drops of organic mint essential oil
3 tablespoons of set honey or raw agave syrup
25g raw cacao butter, melted
100ml of water

Blend all the cream ingredients until smooth.

Continued on next page ...

Pour the mint cream on top of the torte mixture, whilst still in its tin. Refrigerate the torte for at least an hour.

To loosen your torte from the tin, boil a kettle and briefly hold the metal of the cake tin over the steam to warm it. This will melt the raw cacao butter that you greased the tin with earlier.

Slide the torte out of the cake tin and onto a plate (you may need to slide a sharp knife under the cake base to loosen it).

Decoration

raw cacao powder for dusting
mint leaves for decoration

Dust with raw cacao butter and decorate with mint leaves.

Keeps for 48 hours in the fridge, or cut it into slices and freeze it without the mint leaves.

Most people don't know you can use certain essential oils to flavour food. My favourites are mint, lavender, geranium and rose. I use them in raw chocolate, ice-creams and desserts for an added element of sophistication.

Caramel Hazelnut Ice-Cream

This is a sophisticated ice-cream that never fails to impress my non-raw friends and family. If you don't tell them it's raw, they'll never know!

Equipment: blender, muslin or nut milk bag, ice-cream maker or whisk (preferably electrical)
Serves 4

200g hazelnuts, soaked for 8 hours and rinsed
300ml of water
8 medjool dates, pitted
½ teaspoon of vanilla essence or seeds of 1 vanilla pod
1 pinch of mineral salt

Blend the soaked hazelnuts, water, medjool dates, vanilla and mineral salt until finely blended. Strain the mixture through a nut milk or muslin. Chill the mixture in the fridge.

Ice-Cream Maker:

When the mixture is chilled, put it into your ice cream maker to make ice cream.

Keep in a sealed container in the freezer for up to 1 month (although probably not, because you'll have eaten it by then!).*

By Hand:

Put the mixture in the freezer. After 2 hours take it out of the freezer, whisk it to break up the ice crystals, and then put it back in the freezer. Do this every few hours until the mixture is too frozen to whisk. Usually you'll need to do this three or four times over a 6 to 8 hour period.*

* To serve, take your ice-cream out of the freezer and put it in the fridge 20 minutes before you want to eat it. This makes it easier to serve.

Chocolate Orange Mousse

When I created this recipe I couldn't believe how delicious it was! We used to get Chocolate Oranges at Christmas time, so this divine mousse brings back fond childhood memories for me.

Equipment: knife, chopping board, blender, zester
Serves 4

2 avocados, peel and stone removed
5 heaped teaspoons of raw cacao powder
4 tablespoons of raw agave syrup or honey
1 orange, zest
1 orange, for decoration (optional)
1 pinch of mineral salt
seeds from 1 vanilla pod or 1 teaspoon of vanilla essence
200ml of water

Blend all the ingredients until smooth and creamy. Serve your mousse as it is or decorate it with a thin twist of orange.

Keeps for up to 24 hours in the fridge, or freeze it for a delicious chocolate orange ice-cream.

Apple Cakes with Orange Cream

These little beauties are one of my favourite desserts. They look so pretty, and it's worth taking time to cut the decorative apple slices finely and evenly so the apple fan on top looks lovely.

Equipment: knife, chopping board, blender, zester, food processor (optional), chefs rings or a muffin tin
Makes three little 9cm cakes

Cake

200g of grated apple
200g almonds, freshly ground
25g raisins
1 teaspoon of ground cinnamon
1 teaspoon of set honey or raw agave syrup
½ teaspoon of vanilla essence
3 tablespoons of extra virgin coconut oil, melted

Combine all the ingredients, in a food processor if you have one, or in a mixing bowl if you don't. Divide the mixture between three chefs rings, or line a muffin tin with cling film and divide between 4 of the muffin indents. Put your little apple cakes in the freezer to set whilst you make the orange cream.

Orange Cream

100g cashews
1 teaspoon of vanilla essence or the seeds from 1 vanilla pod
½ orange, zest
3 tablespoons of fresh orange juice
1 teaspoon of set honey or raw agave syrup

Blend all the orange cream ingredients together until smooth, adding an extra tablespoon of water at a time if necessary, whilst keeping the cream as thick as possible. Spread the cream on top of your little cakes in their tins, and put them back in the fridge to become firmer.

Continued on next page …

Decoration

1 apple
1 lemon, juice of

Cut the apple into quarters, carefully removing the core. Slice the apple quarters thinly along their length so that you have crescent-shaped pieces. Coat the apple slices in the lemon juice to stop them browning. Remove your little apple cakes from their moulds and arrange the apple slices in a fan across the tops.

Best eaten fresh, but keeps in the fridge for 48 hours. This recipe also freezes well without the apple slices on top.

I used to be a fashion designer, and my love of colour and form has followed me in to the raw food world.

Vanilla Ice-Cream

Whether it's for you or the kids in your life, a stash of vanilla ice-cream in the freezer is always a winner. This raw version makes a beautiful base for a sundae, drizzled with warmed up raw chocolate spread (p.288) and topped with crushed nuts or fresh berries.

Equipment: knife, chopping board, blender, nut milk or jelly bag, ice-cream maker or whisk (preferably electrical)
Serves 8

Almond Cream

300g almonds, preferably soaked overnight and rinsed
600ml of water

Blend the almonds and water together until smooth. Strain the mixture in 3 batches, using a nut milk bag or a clean tea towel, squeezing all the creamy liquid out. This liquid is your almond cream.

Ice-Cream

600ml almond cream
2 vanilla pods
3 tablespoons of vanilla essence
100ml raw agave syrup/honey
¼ cup of extra virgin coconut oil

Cut the vanilla pods in half length ways, and scrape out the tiny black seeds. Blend the vanilla seeds with the rest of the ice cream ingredients.

Chill the mixture in the fridge. When the mixture is chilled, put it into your ice cream maker to make ice cream, or make by hand using the method in the caramel hazelnut ice-cream recipe on p.256. Store in the freezer in an airtight container for up to one month.

Take out of the freezer and put in the fridge 15 minutes before serving.

Sweet Treats & Snacks

'My stash of raw goodies keeps me off the chocolate and biscuits, and means I always have something to offer friends when they come round for a cup of tea.'

Of all the food we eat, the food we snack on is often the unhealthiest. Snacks such as crisps, biscuits or chocolate can seem like a convenient quick fix when we're busy at work and our energy levels start to slump. But the reality is that we pay for that 'convenience' with our health. So, if you make just one positive change to your daily eating habits, replace these sugar and saturated fat-filled snacks with a healthy raw alternative.

If you've spent a lifetime snacking on unhealthy foods it can be difficult to break the habit (I know from my own experience). As you start to make the transition toward eating more healthily, it's important to remember to be gentle with yourself. If you're new to raw food, don't worry about allowing yourself 'too many' raw treats. They are a great transition food, helping you to break any addictions to sugar and saturated fats. Even if you do end up eating a whole batch of them, they're not going to negatively affect your health in the same way eating a big bar of processed chocolate would. As raw food works its magic, you'll find that you naturally eat less raw snacks in one go.

Try replacing your mid-morning bar of chocolate with a rice cake topped with a delicious helping of my raw chocolate spread. And if you feel like having a second and third one - go ahead! This will satisfy your body's craving for something sweet and indulgent, and you won't spend the rest of the day dreaming about the unhealthy alternatives. I've learnt that when it comes to raw food, it's much better to start by setting yourself small achievable goals, rather than taking an all-or-nothing approach. By focusing on making just one small change at a time, you'll be more motivated to keep going.

If you happen to have quite a sweet tooth, or you have kids, or you frequently have a house full of guests, it's a good idea to make sure that you have a generous supply of raw snacks and treats in your fridge or freezer. You can make a batch on the weekend or if you have an evening off during the week. Preparing a selection in advance also means that you can carry some around in your bag for those moments when you feel tired and hungry and are tempted to reach for the coffee and chocolate bars. Most importantly of all, remember that raw food should be fun! So, enjoy sharing these fabulously healthy and guilt-free treats with your family and friends.

Almond Snow Balls

I created these little lovelies as a Christmas treat, but they've become an all-year-round favourite of mine.

Equipment: knife, chopping board, spice grinder or high speed blender
Makes 12-15

250g almonds*, freshly ground
¼ teaspoon of vanilla essence
1 teaspoon of lemon juice
3 tablespoons of raw agave syrup
½ cup of goji berries, finely chopped
3 tablespoons of extra virgin coconut oil, melted

In a bowl, thoroughly combine all the ingredients together. Put the mixture in the fridge for 30 minutes or more to allow the coconut oil to set a bit.

Shape the mixture into balls by rolling about 1 tablespoon of mixture between the palms of your hands.

Decoration

desiccated coconut
goji berries

Scatter a small plate with desiccated coconut and roll your snow balls in the coconut. Finish by pressing a goji berry into the top of each ball.

Keep in the fridge and eat within 10 days, or keep them in the freezer for up to 1 month.

* If you prefer, soak the almonds for 8 hours, then rinse and dehydrate them until completely dry, before grinding them.

Bee Pollen Balls

Bee pollen balls are completely delicious! They are immune-boosting powerhouses too, so if you feel a cold coming on whizz up a batch of these to give your system a boost.

Equipment: food processor, zester
Makes 8 – 10

3 handfuls of almonds, freshly ground
2 tablespoons of bee pollen
2 tablespoons of set honey
½ teaspoon of turmeric
½ orange, zest
3 tablespoons of extra virgin coconut oil
bee pollen, to decorate

Process all the ingredients together in a food processor or by hand.

Take about a tablespoon of mixture and roll into a ball between the palms of your hands. Continue until all the mixture is used up.

Press bee pollen on to the top of each ball to decorate.

These little beauties last in the fridge for a week or in the freezer for a month.

Halva

I love cooked halva, but I love this raw halva even more! It's so incredibly easy to make and you won't believe how utterly delicious it is.

Equipment: food processor
Makes 8-10

1 cup of tahini OR 1 cup of sesame seeds with 1 tablespoon of cold pressed sesame oil
1 cup of raisins
½ teaspoon of vanilla essence or a small piece of vanilla bean
100g sesame seeds, to decorate

In a food processor, process all the ingredients (except the sesame seeds for decorating) until the raisins are thoroughly chopped and evenly mixed through. Shape the halva mixture into whatever shape takes your fancy. I make squares, oblongs or balls.

To finish, scatter the sesame seeds for decorating on a small plate and roll your halva in them until completely covered.

Put your halva in the fridge or freezer to firm up.

These will last for 2 weeks in the fridge or 2 months in the freezer.

Tahini Energy Balls

These little balls of energy are perfect for taking to work or for the kids' lunch boxes. They are full of goodness and taste fantastic to boot.

Equipment: knife, chopping board, food processor
Makes 12-15

2 handfuls of unsulphured dried apricots (the brown kind)
4 dates, pitted
1 handful of hulled hemp seeds
1 handful of pumpkin seeds
1 tablespoon of cinnamon
1 tablespoon of raw cacao powder
1 tablespoon of raw agave syrup/honey
3 tablespoons of tahini (preferably raw)

In a food processor or by hand, chop together the dried apricots, dates and seeds. Add the rest of the ingredients and combine well.

Shape the mixture into balls approximately 2.5cm across.

Decoration

hulled hemp seeds/raw cacao nibs/chopped pumpkin seeds to decorate (optional)

If you want to decorate them, press hulled hemp seeds/raw cacao nibs/pumpkin seeds into the top of each energy ball. Finally, put them in the fridge or freezer to set.

Keeps in the fridge for 2 weeks or in the freezer for 2 months.

Apricot Vanilla Chocolates

If you love Toblerone, you'll love these! They are light and fruity, and they glow with a pale gold light that is very pretty.

Equipment: knife, chopping board, bain-marie*, chocolate moulds (optional)
Makes 30-36

100g raw cacao butter
1 tablespoon of extra virgin coconut oil
5 tablespoons of raw cacao powder
100g almonds, freshly ground
3 tablespoons of raw agave syrup
1 teaspoon of vanilla essence
100g unsulphured dried apricots, finely chopped

Melt the raw cacao butter and coconut oil over a bain-marie*. Then stir in the remaining ingredients until thoroughly combined.

Pour the chocolate mixture into chocolate moulds** and allow to set somewhere cool, or in the fridge.

* A bain-marie is a double-boiler set up for melting your raw cacao butter and coconut oil without cooking it. You can buy bain-maries but I just use a large soup bowl that sits comfortably on top of a straight sided soufflé dish.   A bowl on top of a smaller saucepan works well too. The soufflé dish or saucepan holds hot water and the soup bowl warms up over the top.

** If you don't have chocolate moulds, place greaseproof paper on a plate and dollop teaspoons of the soft chocolate onto the paper.

Chocolate Coconut Dreams

These delicious raw treats are inspired by the dark chocolate Bounty bars that we get here in the UK. They were my favourite when I was a kid, so I decided to create this delicious version, refined sugar-free and raw.

Equipment: bain-marie (see p.278), cupcake tray
Makes 12

Centres

10g raw cacao butter
3 tablespoons of extra virgin coconut oil
150g desiccated coconut
1½ teaspoons of vanilla essence
1 tablespoon of raw agave syrup

Melt the raw cacao butter and coconut oil together over a bowl of hot water (bain-marie).

When your fats have melted, mix in the dessicated coconut, vanilla essence and raw agave syrup.

Line a shallow cupcake tray with cling film. Divide your coconut mixture evenly around the tray and press it down firmly. Put the tray in the freezer so your mixture can set.

Continued on next page ...

Chocolate Coating

50g raw cacao powder
50g raw cacao butter
1 tablespoon of extra virgin coconut oil
1 teaspoon of vanilla essence
4 tablespoons of raw agave syrup
1 pinch of mineral salt

Melt the raw cacao and extra virgin coconut oils over a bowl of hot water (bain-marie). Mix in the other ingredients thoroughly. Remove the chocolate from the bain-marie and allow the mixture to cool a bit, so it doesn't melt the coconut mixture in the next stage.

When your chocolate has cooled but is still spreadable, take out your firm coconut bars and cover them with the chocolate, using a small spatula or smooth knife. Place the coconut bars on a plate or flat baking tray.

Once you have coated all the bars, put them in the fridge until the chocolate has set.

Keeps in the fridge for 2 weeks or the freezer for 2 months.

Orange Cinnamon Truffles

This is a classic chocolate combination that works really well with almonds. I keep them in the fridge and bring them out when friends come round for tea.

Equipment: bain-marie (see p.278), spice-grinder or blender, zester
Makes 15 – 20

75g raw cacao butter
5 tablespoons of raw cacao powder
200g almonds, freshly ground
4 tablespoons of raw agave syrup
1 tablespoon of ground cinnamon
½ orange, zest of
1 tablespoon of bee pollen (optional)
bee pollen/cinnamon/orange zest to decorate (optional)

Melt the raw cacao butter over a bain-marie. When the butter has melted, stir in the remaining ingredients (apart from anything you're using to decorate them with later) until thoroughly combined.

Allow the mixture to cool and set slightly. When it's firm enough, roll the truffle mixture into balls. On a firm surface, press your thumb firmly into the centre of each ball, flattening it and creating an indentation. Sprinkle with any decoration you are using, and put in the fridge or freezer to set.

Keeps for 2 weeks in the fridge or 2 months in the freezer.

Lime Spread

Both refreshing and creamy, this spread is delicious on raw crackers, rice cakes or apple slices for breakfast or as a snack. It's made with fresh lime so it needs to be eaten within a couple of days, but that shouldn't be a problem because it's so moorish.

Equipment: knife, chopping board, blender, zester
Makes enough for a few days, unless you're feeding your family with it!

100g cashew nuts
1 ½ limes, zest of + 2 tablespoons of juice
2 tablespoons of set honey or raw agave syrup
50ml of water

Blend all your ingredients until smooth. Store in a jar in the fridge and eat within 2 days.

Chocolate Spread

With a jar of this chocolate spread in the fridge, you always have an instant sweet fix at hand. Just remember not to eat it late at night if you want to get any sleep!

Equipment: bain-marie (see p.278)
Makes enough to fill a 200ml jar

½ cup of extra virgin coconut oil
6 tablespoons of raw cacao powder
6 tablespoons of raw agave syrup
1 teaspoon of vanilla essence
1 pinch of mineral salt

Melt the coconut oil in a bowl over just-boiled water (a bain-marie). Stir in the remaining ingredients and mix it until it's all smooth. Spoon your chocolate spread into a clean container or jar for storage.

Eat your raw chocolate spread with apple slices, raw crackers or rice cakes.

Keeps for up to 2 months in the fridge.

Index

What Saskia's clients say about working with her

'*Coaching with Saskia set me off on an incredible journey of self-empowerment. Saskia coached me towards real clarity, inspiring me to take back my power, to spread my wings and to really become the best of myself.*' Deborah Stanley

'*She shines her light and energy through her teaching and through the way she is. She inspires you, but more importantly believes you have it in you to do the same.*' Andrea Giles

'*I feel transformed. I have shifted years of bad eating patterns and feel as though I am truly honouring the skin I'm in rather than using it as a waste disposal unit. My experience was one of physical lightening, emotional balancing and clarification on countless levels. I would recommend working with Saskia to everyone.*' Bethan Stritton

Further information

If you'd like to discover more about the Raw freedom approach to falling in love with life, please visit Saskia's website at www.rawfreedom.co.uk

When you join Saskia's mailing list you'll also receive downloadable gifts as well as her newsletter 'The Raw Path to Freedom'. Through her motivational emails she shares many more quick, easy and delicious raw food recipes as well as practical raw food tips and life inspiration. To join Saskia's mailing list visit www.rawfreedom.co.uk

If you're ready and excited to find out more about getting coaching support from Saskia, then please book a telephone or Skype consultation via her online diary www.rawfreedomdiary.com

You can also connect with Saskia here:

www.facebook.com/SaskiaFraser
www.twitter.com/SaskiaFraser

Lightning Source UK Ltd.
Milton Keynes UK
UKOW07f1336190216

268733UK00005B/20/P